Attitude, Ability and the 80-20 Rule

The Makings of Exceptional Performers

by

Carl Van

Author of
The 8 Characteristics of the Awesome Adjuster
and *Gaining Cooperation*

INTERNATIONAL INSURANCE INSTITUTE, INC.

Written by Carl van Lamsweerde
Book interior design and layout by Ann van Lamsweerde
Edited by Ann van Lamsweerde
Cover and all interior illustrations by Mike Shapiro, CartoonResource.com

First Edition

Copyright ©2011 International Insurance Institute, Inc.
2112 Belle Chasse Hwy. #11-319
Gretna, LA 70056
T: 504-393-4570
T: 888-414-8811
www.insuranceinstitute.com

Published by International Insurance Institute, Inc.
ISBN: 1461052947
ISBN-13: 9781461052944
Printed in Charleston, SC.

For my genius daughter,
Amanda van Lamsweerde,
who keeps teaching me
*how the brain **really** works.*

8-9-11

RYAN,

HOPE YOU DON'T MIND ME
USING A CONVERSATION WE HAD. I
HAD TO ALTER IT A LITTLE, BUT
IT'S PRETTY CLOSE. ENJOY

CARL VAN

Pg 93

ACKNOWLEDGEMENTS

Without the support of some key customers, I would never have had the time or opportunity to write this book. I'd like to take the time to thank these especially loyal customers for their extraordinary support over the last few years:

Mike Day, Tresa Edwards, Chuck Eldredge – Rural Community Insurance Services

Gerry Wilson, Hal Belodoff, Jim Tignanelli, Rick Adam, Rich Mariani, Karen Stickel, Glenn Basko, Joe Carey – Plymouth Rock

Debra Hinz, Dianne Cohen, Rebecca Hughes – Macro Pro
Jill Kilroy, Twanna Amos, Dennis Bianchi – Horace Mann
Peter Strauss, Rick Duane – Montana State Fund
Irene Bianchi, Sandi Halpert – RSA Insurance
Roger Kaage – Rockford Mutual
Troy Bourassa - Alberta Motor Association
Jeff Suloff – Mountain West Mutual
Deborah Wolfenbarger - AllCat Claims Services
Grace Thomas, Paul Gary, Jane Eaton – Great American
Eddie Gainey, Dale Vonderluft – Foremost
Karel Davis, Lainie Barrows – State Comp Ins. Fund
Ted Duckworth – Germania
Paul Colandreo – Liberty Mutual
Lesley Kochel – Sedgwick

THANKS

Thanks
To Jack and everyone at ICGLink who help keep all my web pages organized and running smoothly. To Mark Williams and the good folks at AlphaGraphics who make all of my Marketing materials look so good. And to Shannon, Nikki, Renee and the whole UPS gang who print, organize and ship at least a mountain of my documents weekly.

Special Thanks
As always, a special thanks to my father, John Martin. Who not only continues to support all of my business efforts, but having raised me with a desire to help others, continues to support me with his invaluable guidance whenever I need it.

Very Special Thanks
Very special thanks to my beautiful wife, Ann van Lamsweerde, who is always there for me. Not only is she supportive, but she has the greatest inner strength of anyone I have ever known. Despite difficult times, the murder of her brother and hurricane Katrina, she remains kind, generous and always gracious. I admire her beyond words.

ABOUT THE AUTHOR

Carl Van was born Carl Christian Gregory Maria Baron van Lamsweerde. He was the second son of a prominent Dutch noble and artist, Franciscus Ludovicus Aloysius Maria Baron van Lamsweerde.

After the death of Carl's father at the age of 11, his mother, Joyce, married John E. Martin. Mr. Martin was a successful business owner and investor. Mr. Martin had tremendous influence over Carl, recapping stories of coming to America with virtually nothing and building a successful business. Carl admired his new father greatly, and marveled at his generosity.

Carl had a remarkable resemblance to his father Franz, and was greatly influenced by John. His mother would often comment, "I look at Carl and I see Franz. Then he starts to talk, and out comes John."

Carl worked his way through college, taking years of night school to earn his degree in Insurance. By the time he earned his degree, Carl was already a Regional Claims Manager, and even writing and teaching several IEA courses.

With his first marriage, came his daughter Amanda Elaine Denise Baroness van Lamsweerde, who Carl continuously proclaims is a child genius.

Carl married Ann Elizabeth Wimsatt, on July 16, 1994, and together they have lived in Sacramento, CA, Nashville, TN, and now reside in New Orleans, LA. In April of 1998, Carl sold his house, cashed in his retirement, and gambled it all on the idea that insurance companies would be interested in meaningful, real-life claims training. He created International Insurance Institute, Inc. a company dedicated to the enhancement of the insurance claims industry, and now widely considered the single best claims training company in the United States and Canada.

Carl Van has dedicated his life to studying how people think and interact, and has developed classes and programs to improve the success of individuals as well business groups.

I have known Carl since we met in kindergarten, and even back then in our school days. Carl looked out for people. Obviously, Carl was honing his skills that he uses today. It only takes a few minutes in his presence to know how passionately he believes that the greatest thing a person can do in this life, is be of service to someone in need. That, he insists, is the opportunity most of us have every single day.

In this book, Carl shares his wit, wisdom, knowledge and sixth sense of dealing with people. He's a great friend and an inspiration. I hope you find this book as valuable in your world as Carl has been in mine.

- Steve Belkin
Open All Nite Entertainment

TABLE OF CONTENTS

CHAPTER SONG REFERENCES

Song	Performer	Album	Written By
Sympathy for the Devil	The Rolling Stones	Beggars Banquet	Mick Jagger, Keith Richards
Fast Car	Tracey Chapman	Tracey Chapman	Tracey Chapman
Nothing But Flowers	Talking Heads	Naked	David Byrne
Life During Wartime	Talking Heads	Fear of Music	David Byrne
King Tut	Steve Martin	King Tut (single)	Steve Martin
Man on the Moon	R.E.M.	Automatic for The People	Bill Berry, Peter Buck, Mike Mills, Michael Stipe
Goodbye Stranger	Supertramp	Breakfast in America	Rick Davies, Roger Hodgson
I am Woman	Helen Reddy	I Am Woman	Ray Burton, Helen Reddy
Mrs. Potter's Lullaby	Counting Crows	The Desert Life	Adam Duritz
Thing Called Love	Bonnie Raitt	Nick of Time	John Hiatt
Middle of the Road	Pretenders	Learning to Crawl	Chrissie Hynde
Diamonds on the Soles of Her Shoes	Paul Simon	Graceland	Joseph Shabalala, Paul Simon

Song	Performer	Album	Written By
Soak up the Sun	Sheryl Crow	C'mon C'mon	Sheryl Crow, Jeff Trott
Burning Down the House	Talking Heads	Speaking in Tongues	David Byrne, Chris Frantz, Jerry Harrison, Tina Weymouth
Bad Moon Rising	Credence Clearwater Revival	Green River	John Fogerty
Mmm, Mmm, Mmm, Mmm	Crash Test Dummies	God Shuffled His Feet	Brad Roberts
Mmm Bop	Hansen	Middle of Nowhere	Isaac Hanson
Always Look on the Bright Side of Life	Monty Python	Monty Python's Life of Brian	Eric idle
Don't Worry, Be Happy	Bobby McFerrin	Simple Pleasures	Bobby McFerrin
Beautiful	Carole King	Tapestry	Carole King
Breakout	Swing Out Sister	It's Better to Travel	Andy Connell, Corinne Drewery, Martin Jackson
Here's Where the Story Ends	The Sundays	Reading, Writing and Arithmetic	Harriet Wheeler

Allow Me to Introduce Myself

Please allow me to introduce myself;
I'm a man of wealth and taste.
"Sympathy for the Devil" – Rolling Stones

Well, not really much wealth, and according to my wife, little or no taste (at least when it comes to furniture). But I do consider myself a trainer, course designer, and coach . . . not a writer. So please, forgive me if during this book, I slip in and out of my trainer mode and; instead of just commenting on what Exceptional Performers do, I actually try to teach.   Just be glad I don't have a flip chart.

I prefer to talk to people rather than to write to them. I love the phone and hate e-mail. This is why I have chosen to write this book in this particular style, as if I am talking to someone. I will refer to you, the reader, of this book without having any idea who you are or what you do. That is to simply help me convey the concepts without tuning out. It helps me if I pretend I'm talking to someone rather than writing to that person.

I mention this because I wouldn't want anyone to get mad at me and say to themselves, "What is he talking about, I don't do that." Just know that when I refer to "you," I'm talking to those of you who see the need for improvement and want help.

I freely use the word "we" throughout this book, because I want you to know I consider myself someone, like you, who wants to improve. No matter what project I may be working on, or any business endeavor I may be involved in, I NEVER forget that I am seeking improvement for myself, and never want anyone else to forget it either. After all, I am not writing this book for the upper echelon of management; I am writing it for those of us who consider ourselves employees. So I hope nobody minds that I fight to stay in the club.

Another thing you should know when reading this book, is that in most cases when I use names for customers and employees, those are not the actual names of those employees and/or customers. They are the names of friends and family members. I decided this might increase the chance that people might read this book if they knew their name was in it.

However, when I refer to actual Exceptional Performers and use first and last name, rest assured that these people are real, and are out there right now being exceptional. Some have since moved into management, and others love their jobs so much they stay right where they are.

Admission #1: I am not a researcher. You should know that I did not conduct formal research. I have no control groups to test out my theories, and no written documentation to substantiate each and every hypothesis. What I do offer is practical experience and examples to better illustrate how to gain cooperation. After 30+ years in the business world, years of management and executive experience, 15+ years of monitoring phone calls, designing training programs, and facilitating over 1,000 workshops, I have a certain perspective about what one can do to become an Exceptional Performer. That is what I am relying upon, so don't expect to find me in some Management Journal. I'm not there. I'm here, trying to help.

Admission #2: I'm an Insurance guy. My background in the business world comes from the insurance claims industry, as does much of my management experience, so I will hope you forgive me if I use the insurance industry as a backdrop to illustrate my point with real-life situations. Regardless of the type of business you may be in, I am sure you will agree that the lessons learned can apply to almost anyone.

Admission #3: I'm Lazy. (Probably has something to do with Admission #1) My first book, *The 8 Characteristics of* *the Awesome Adjuster*, was quite successful in the claims world. Ever since its release, I have been bombarded with people telling me the skills, characteristics, and attitudes that make great claims people mentioned in the book are completely transferable to almost any industry. After years of people telling me that I should rewrite it with a more general outlook, I finally agreed. That book is called, *The 8 Characteristics of the Awesome Employee.*

I dedicated quite a large section of that book to Attitude and Ability, and decided to give that information its own platform, and now we have <u>this</u> book. Is that lazy or what? Yes, the information is the same, the names are the same, and even the titles of the chapters are the same. Lazy!

Admission #4: I have a terrible memory. I want to tell you that <u>every</u> <u>single</u> story I tell in the book about me, things I have witnessed, things people have said to me are absolutely true!

Well, mostly true. Probably all except two…MAYBE three. Which three? I'm not telling you. You see, although I have every intention of telling the truth, or at least the truth as I remember it, I don't intend to sit on The Daily Show or The Today Show someday trying to justify every little detail. This way, if I'm caught exaggerating, or challenged by one of my previous managers that I make fun of, I can just say, "That's one of the three."

Admission #5: I hate being sued. So, throughout this book, I am going to refer to people by name. Sometimes they're real people with their real names or real people and with fake names. Sometimes, I might even make up a fake person and a fake name.

I might be telling a story from a prior article, book, magazine, or even video presentation. I might tell the exact same story but with two different people's names. The reason for that is very simple. Sometimes I use fake names because I don't want to get sued. Would you want to get sued? No, of course you wouldn't. And neither do I. If I do make any money off of this book, I certainly don't want to spend it on legal fees defending myself against some idiot because I've used his real name in a book. So, for the most part, I will probably be using fake names.

However, there will be times when I use real people and their real names. Those times will probably be when I give you both their first and last name. So when I refer to someone by their whole name, you can be assured that these people really exist and the stories are somewhat accurate, at least as best I remember.

So, if you happen to read an article I wrote a number of years ago and I am telling a story and I use a different person's name, don't get your undies in a bunch. It's just what I do. I just like to use names because referring to people as "my manager," "my co-worker," "my partner," all the time can become a little monotonous. So just bear with me and come along for the ride.

❖ ❖ ❖

PART 1

Attitude is Performance

CHAPTER 1

Be Someone

I had a feeling that I belonged;
I had a feeling that I could be someone.
"Fast Car" – Tracey Chapman

You want to Be Someone? Start with attitude.

Attitude is such a huge issue; I am going to dedicate two sections to it. The first, "Attitude is Performance." The second, "Attitude is Job Satisfaction."

The most important characteristic of an exceptional performer is attitude. However, many people misunderstand attitude, what it is, what it means, and how to alter it. Most people think having a good attitude is being happy all of the time. "Hey, I got 15 assignments on a Friday afternoon! Thanks boss! Thank you sir, may I have another!"

No, attitude for performance doesn't mean being happy all of the time. It means, do you have the right attitude for your job? Do you understand your real role, and how important you are? Do you appreciate how crucial it is that you do an outstanding job? THIS is what I am talking about. Performance is 80% attitude and 20% ability.

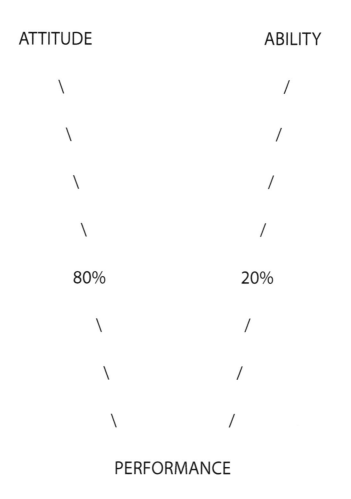

ATTITUDE   ABILITY

80%   20%

PERFORMANCE

When I say that performance is 80% attitude, again, I don't mean being happy all of the time. I mean that your performance; how good you are at your job, will be determined 80% by your attitude about what you think your job is, and the other 20% by your ability to do that job.

It's the old 80-20 rule in action-"The Pareto Principle."

CHAPTER 2

Covered with Flowers

There was a factory, now there are mountains and rivers.
There was a shopping mall, now it's all covered with flowers.
If this is paradise, I wish I had a lawn mower.
"Nothing but Flowers" – Talking Heads

The Pareto Principle

Vilfedo Pareto was an Italian economist who observed in 1906 that 80% of the land in Italy was owned by 20% of the population. Pareto himself developed the concept of the "Pareto Efficiency" in the context of the distribution of income and wealth among the population. It spawned the rule of thumb in business known as the 80-20 rule. Business management expert Joseph Juran suggested the 80-20 rule and named it after Vilfedo Pareto. Nice guy!

The 80-20 rule (the Pareto Principle), basically states that, for many events, roughly 80% of the effects come from 20% of the causes. Marketing experts say that "80% of your sales come from 20% of your clients." Criminologists tell us "80% of the crime is caused by 20% of the people." In my Time Management classes we teach that "80% of the results you produce will take only 20% of your time." Heck, I've even heard fashion people say "You wear 20% of your clothes, 80% of the time." It seems like everybody has an 80-20 rule.

Well, here is my 80-20 rule: ***People's performance is 80% attitude and 20% ability***. I am not sure if I made it up, or I heard it somewhere. Maybe it's just a variation of the old saying, "Success is 80% attitude and 20% aptitude." So, maybe I just changed "success" to "performance" and "aptitude" to "ability" in a dream I had. Who knows? I looked it up on the internet and the only other reference I could find on performance is 80% attitude, and 20% ability was an article I wrote entitled, "Lessons in Customer Service and Attitude."

In his book, *The Psychology of Selling*, Joe Love says, "80% of the success of top salespeople is due to their winning attitude. Only 20% is aptitude. Since sales performance is 80% mental attitude, this winning edge is psychological." So maybe he gets the credit. I know that Brian Tracey, in his book *The Psychology of Achievement,* certainly talks about it a lot. Okay, so maybe I didn't invent it. But I sure preach it enough!

So until Oprah hauls me in and confronts me with the fact that it has been said by at least 173 people before me, I'm calling it, "The Carl Van attitude-performance-ability super incredible correlation principle ratio effect." Or, let's call it "The Van Principle" for short. I would have called it "The Van Factor," but I already invented that years ago. Never heard of it? Sure. I'm known all over the world for it. Basically, The Van Factor says *that when you are teaching a class or giving a speech, you take a look around the room. You divide the number of people with their legs crossed by the total number of people in the room. When that number hits 30%, you'd better take a break.*

All right, back to the 80-20 rule.

A great example of performance is 80% attitude and 20% ability is a story about an interaction I had with a flight attendant one day. I've been threatening for years to dedicate an entire book to something she said to me. I'll never forget those four words several years ago. The four words that I've used as an example at almost every speech I give on customer service. I can still remember the day that Sweet Dee said to me, "Oh her? She's new!"

CHAPTER 3

This Ain't No Disco

*This ain't no party; this ain't no disco;
this ain't no fooling around.
No time for dancing, or lovey dovey.
I ain't got time for that now.*
"Life during Wartime" – Talking Heads

Oh, her? She's New

I promised you a story about, "Oh, her? She's new." Well, here it is.

I fly all the time, as part of my job. Every week I'm on a plane going somewhere. My nickname is Carl "Moving" Van. So I have a fairly veteran perspective of the customer service I get on planes. I fly so much I usually get bumped up to first class just for flying. I hardly need to use my miles to upgrade anymore.

Now first class is nice, but it's not like on *Seinfeld* where they put little slippers on you and serve you hot fudge sundaes or anything. But it's usually pretty comfortable.

One day, several years ago, I was sitting in first class and there was this somewhat overbearing flight attendant. My favorite T.V. show is *It's Always Sunny in Philadelphia*. So we'll call her Sweet Dee.

Sweet Dee was being very pushy, telling people what to do. "Close that laptop." "Put that up there." "Put that seatbelt on." "That can't go there." "That has to be turned off." She wasn't really asking people, she was just ordering them around, in a demanding, unnecessarily authoritative tone. At some point, this really started to bug me, and I couldn't resist. I finally said to her, "You know, I think your customer service skills could really use some improvement." Of course the other passengers were all nervous looking around at each other thinking, "Ooooooo…. he's gonna get it"

"Well sir," she said snidely, "I'm here mainly for your safety."

Ah, that's all I needed to know. With that statement she answered my question on how someone in the customer service business could be so lacking in skills. The answer is she's not lacking. Her ability is just fine.

If you fly as much as I do, you know that pilots say this all of the time, right? "The flight attendants are here mainly for your safety, but if there is something they can do to make you feel more comfortable, please feel free to ask…." You've heard that right? Well, Sweet Dee actually believes this!

So, let me pose a question: What's driving her performance? She knows how to be polite if she wants to. She knows she's a representative of the airline. She probably has to deal with huffy customers every day. So what's driving her poor customer service performance? This poor woman thinks she's in the <u>safety</u> business. She doesn't know she's in the customer service business. She believes her job is safety. She even said it, "I'm here mainly for your safety." What's driving her poor performance? Her attitude!

And her attitude is: *I'm not here for your pleasure. I'm not here for your comfort. I'm not even here to ever make sure you come back again. I'm here for your safety.* And because of that, she can be mean. She can be nasty. She can be bossy. Why? Because she's not in the customer service business, she's in the safety business. And because of her attitude, she is perfectly okay with pushing customers around.

So, I responded, "Yes, I agree you are here for safety. But you're not in the safety business. You are in the customer service business. You see, I think you made a mistake by separating the two. Safety is <u>part</u> of the customer service you provide. It's an important part, but still just a part."

As she rolled her eyes, I continued, "Think about it. 99.9 percent of the time, you are dealing with people and their needs; Serving drinks, answering their questions, and getting them things. You're not dealing with safety issues. Most of your time on the job is spent providing customer service." I said to her, "Flying is very safe, as you know."

I even asked her, "Have you ever been on a plane that's crashed?" "No," she replied. "Well, there you go then," I said, "You've never even been **on** a plane that's crashed. Yet it's your excuse for bossing people around." Again, she demanded, "I'm here mainly for your safety…SIR!"

I was getting tired of this conversation. Noticing that all of the passengers had pulled their ear phones out and were listening intently to the conversation, I finally said, "Okay. You're here mainly for my safety. Fine then, why is the other flight attendant back in coach being so nice? You know, the one who is always smiling? Why is she being polite? Why is she being courteous, helpful, and friendly? Why is she asking people to do things and not barking orders? She's doing the same job you are, yet she's making people feel good about it. Why is that?"

Sweet Dee looked down the aisle, looked back at me, smiled at me condescendingly, pointed down at the other flight attendant, and said, "Oh, her? She's new."

There you have it. A perfect example of someone who's attitude is driving their performance. Was it her ability? Probably not, she knows how to smile. She knows how to ask instead of demand. She knows how to talk to people, so as not to make them feel yelled at. Her ability is just fine. What was driving her poor performance in customer service? Her attitude!

It's her attitude about what she does for a living which is driving her poor performance. Maybe her attitude is that she is in the safety business. Maybe her attitude is that she is in the transportation business. Maybe her attitude is that she is in the "keeping the airplane clean" business. Who knows?

It's not that she has a nasty attitude in life. It's just that she doesn't understand her job. You see, in my opinion, she's not in the transportation business. She's not in the safety business. She's in the customer service business. Performance is 80% attitude and 20% ability.

Want another example? Fine, meet Jerome.

CHAPTER 4

Line up Just to See Him

Now if I'd known, they'd line up just to see him,
I'd taken all my money, and bought me a museum.
"King Tut" – Steve Martin

People line up just to see Jerome. To tell you about Jerome, I have to get back to air travel. Some people hate to travel. But generally, I like it. I've been traveling virtually every week for years now, delivering customer service courses to people all over the U.S., Canada and now the U.K.

Like most people, I don't care too much for the security lines at the airport. I don't like delays, don't get excited about the food on the planes, and don't relish the time spent picking up my rental car. Other than that, travel isn't too bad. I certainly enjoy the opportunity to see a number of places most people don't get the chance to see. So, overall, the plusses outweigh the minuses.

One aspect of traveling that normally would be considered one of those minuses is checking in baggage. However, I'm going to talk about how it has become a plus. But first, I would like to take a moment to explain the connection all of this has to do with the exceptional performers. Well, most of us are in the customer service business, in some capacity.

We all know sometimes customers can be difficult. Perhaps they are frustrated, nervous, or in a hurry. We accept that most of the time, if we do our jobs well, we can take away some of the pain our customers are experiencing by doing an exceptional job in handling their situation.

To the degree that we dedicate ourselves to delivering truly exceptional customer service, we can make their experience a much better process. In my travels, I sometimes come across individuals who are so completely committed to customer service, it surprises me.

Back to my example: As a proud resident of New Orleans, I fly out of the New Orleans Louis Armstrong International Airport. I always check my bags with the skycaps because I have so much training material I bring along with me.

One day a couple of years ago, I pulled up to the skycap station and noticed that most of the skycaps were doing what they always do; they were standing behind their booths, waiting for us passengers to drag our bags up to them. Once there, they would ask that question that is so consistent among skycaps that I assume they must receive weeks of intensive training. The ritualistic, "Where are you traveling to?" Well, nothing wrong with that, that's their job.

Every so often, I would run across a skycap who would break from his rigid training and ask, "Where you traveling to…today?" But that didn't occur too often.

On this particular day, however, I saw a skycap actually going out to people's cars to help bring in their luggage. I thought this must be some kind of new service they were offering because I hadn't seen that level of assistance in a long time. He was smiling, shaking hands with people, and generally looking like he was enjoying helping people. So, of course, I thought to myself, "Oh, he must be new."

By pure chance, when I got up to the stand, the person who was going to help me was leaving, and the skycap that was running out to people's cars came in to assist. His named was Jerome Gooden. As I waited for him to ask that question, I was surprised when he said, "Thank you so much for flying with us. Can I ask you where you are flying today, so I can help take care of you?"

Being a little thrown by his enthusiasm for something as mundane as checking luggage, I must have paused for a moment before answering. Because before I could say anything, he asked, "I think I've seen you here before. Do you fly a lot?"

I was floored. Keep in mind I travel every week. I see the same counter people, gift shop people, and even flight attendants virtually every week. This was the first and <u>only</u> person who ever noticed me as a repeat customer and said something to me about it.

Astonished that Jerome had actually noticed that I fly frequently, I could only nod up and down for a moment. He asked my name and looked it up. That's when he said something that really took me by surprise.

He said, "Mr. Van, I'll tell you what. If you travel a lot, you must be a busy person. My name is Jerome. Here is my cell phone number. The next time you are on your way to the airport, give me a call, and I can have everything ready for you." Now a little stunned and becoming suspicious, I started looking around for the hidden camera. "He must be *really* new," I thought to myself.

I asked, "Are you serious?" Jerome replied, "Sure. I don't want you wasting time. Just call me and I'll take care of you." (I know you don't believe this. But it's true. Remember that article I mentioned, "Lessons in Customer Service and Attitude"? It's about Jerome!)

Sure enough, the next time I was on my way to the airport, at 5:20 am, I called Jerome on his cell phone. He answered! He asked me how many bags I had to check and, of course, where I was traveling. When I arrived at the airport and pulled up near the skycap booth, Jerome came out to my car, pulled the bags out of the trunk, put the tags on them, and put them on his cart. He then came up to my window, checked my ID (because that is required), and handed me my tickets. I never even got out of my car. Now THAT'S service!

One time when I called Jerome on my way to the airport, it rolled into voicemail. His outgoing message said, "Hello, this is Jerome. Leave me a message and I'll get right back to you. And remember, the only difference between a good day and a bad day is your attitude." There it is the attitude connection again!

Jerome is one of those rare people who can make a normally negative experience into a pleasant one. Now, when I pull up with my bags, I genuinely look forward to the few moments Jerome and I get to chat before I have to leave. Because my wife travels with me frequently, he knows her as well. When I travel alone, he will say, "Say hi to the first lady Miss Ann for me."

When I asked him if his special service slows him down, he told me that he actually puts many more customers through than if he just waits for people to come to the booth, because he does the computer work in advance.

So in this case, as with many situations, providing outstanding customer service actually takes less time and makes the job easier and much more satisfying.

Can we chalk up all of this enthusiasm to just being new? Jerome is actually a supervisor and has been with his company for over 20 years. He said he got into this job because he loves interacting with people and going out of his way to help them. He says he loves "spending quality time with my beautiful wife Felicia of 20 years and my daughters Jerlicia and Jenesha." He sees a direct connection between his desire to provide a good life for his family and his drive to always find ways to improve the customer's experience.

Jerome commented, "I see the relationships I have formed with people in this job as a significant accomplishment. I have customers who are now friends, who have been as good to me as people I have known all of my life. I found this out after Hurricane Katrina. I received so many calls from people who only know me because I help when they travel. They were checking to see if I was okay, and that really touched my heart."

Jerome is a great example of someone who not only delivers great customer service, but because of his attitude, seems to enjoy his job very much. I'm sure it is profitable for him, as well, because I am sure that most people he shows a special interest in, like me, are more generous when it comes to tips.

Incredibly, during excessively busy times when the airport is packed, I've actually seen people line up to have Jerome help them even when there were other skycaps who weren't busy, just because they wanted to deal with Jerome.

By the way, have I mentioned that performance is 80% attitude, and 20% ability? (Something to chew on)

Speaking of something to chew on, let me take you to the best restaurant in town.

CHAPTER 5

The List

Let's play twister, let's play risk.
See you in heaven if you make the list.
"Man on the Moon" – R.E.M.

The Best Restaurant in Town

As you read this, think about whether or not the two people I describe are good employees.

While on vacation in Florida with my wife, Ann, we wanted to find a nice restaurant to enjoy dinner. Our hotel gave us the name of a nice place and told us it was always packed, because it was, "the best restaurant in town." The concierge offered to make a reservation for us so we wouldn't have to wait. When we got there, we were greeted by a hostess.

"Hi, party of two under Van, please" I said, expectantly. "You are not on the list," the hostess replied.

Confused, I asked, "Are you sure? We are staying right around the corner and the concierge said he made a reservation for us."

The hostess pretended to look the reservation list up and down before saying, "Yes, I'm sure you're not on the list, but we will try to fit you in eventually."

My wife and I sat down by the hostess stand. The clock moved slowly. A half-hour later, I decided it wasn't worth it. "We are tired of waiting, is there any place else you can recommend?" I asked the hostess, who was beginning to get annoyed.

"I'm sorry we don't do that here," she replied, "If you don't mind waiting a bit longer, I'm sure something will become available." "No, we were hungry when we walked in and we are still hungry," I told her. "I'm sure we will be able to find somewhere else, even though we are unfamiliar with this city." "Good luck," the hostess said with a satisfied grin on her pursed lips.

My wife and I walked out with our stomach's growling and were approached by the valet. "Leaving so soon?" he asked. "Yeah, our hotel said they made reservations for us but apparently we weren't on the hostesses' list," I told him.

The valet looked at me, genuinely recognizing our disappointment. "Oh, I'm so sorry," he said. "Let me recommend another place for you. It's also nice and maybe they will have room for you tonight." The valet took his cell phone, called another restaurant and told them he had a customer here who couldn't get a table tonight, because his restaurant is full. He asked them if they could accommodate a party of two under the name "Van."

"All right, they said they would be happy to take you in about ten minutes," the valet said with a smile. "Let me give you the directions." I looked at him in disbelief. "Thanks, that's more help than we were expecting after speaking with the hostess," I told him and shook his hand. "No problem, it's my job," he said. "I'll be right back with your car."

Okay, so how did the hostess do? How did the valet do? Are they good employees? What do you think the difference is between these two people? Is it ability or attitude?

Give both of these individuals an opportunity to impress a customer; even though they both can, one will, and the other won't...

CHAPTER 6

Some They Do

Now some they do, and some they don't;
and some you just can't tell.
And some they will, and some they won't;
with some it's just as well.
"Goodbye Stranger" – Supertramp

Will everyone give it their best shot to improve? No, not really. Some will and some won't. How can you tell?

A lot of people ask me if there are some quick easy dividing lines between the truly exceptional performer and everybody else. And the answer to that is yes, there are some. I will give you an example.

When I teach my classes, whether it be Customer Service, Time Management, or Negotiation classes, I like to start off in the class by letting them know that they will be doing role-plays. I will say to the group, "We will be doing role-plays today, and you will be earning points and competing today for prizes. At the end of the day, we will have a winning team."

I get a lot of bored, blank stares until I tell them that they will be competing for cash and prizes.

I will ask the group, "Who here hates role-plays? Raise your hand." Usually people will raise their hands and the first person who raises their hand, I point to them and say, "Okay, you'll be first." It's always fun to give them a taste of my teaching style right off the bat.

But in any case, I break them up into teams. I tell them that they will be doing role-plays, and that they are going to have to pick a team captain. I warn them, "The team captain is going to play a very important part regarding role-plays today, so pick a good one."

I give them 30 seconds to pick a team captain, and of course everyone points around at each other at the table. "You be team captain, you were here last." "No, you be team captain, you have the most experience." "Hey, Steve should be team captain, he's got a pen." You know the usual stuff. I've even had people on teams playing Rock-Paper-Scissors trying to get out of it.

After about 30 seconds I'll ask, "Okay, did everybody pick a team captain? Please raise your hand if you're a team captain." When I look around the room, the people who have their hands raised are usually pretty disgruntled and don't look too happy. Every once in a while, I'll have someone who got picked as team captain raise a particular finger a little higher than the rest.

At this point, I ask them, "Tell me, do you have a stressful job?" Virtually everyone, regardless of their business, will say yes. But then I ask them this, "Of the stress that you feel during the day, what percentage of that stress you believe is self induced?" And often people will say, "50%," or "80%," or, sometimes even, "90%."

I strongly believe that it follows the 80-20 rule. That 80% of the stress we feel is self induced. Now, what I don't mean to say is that we have control over things that cause us stress. I believe strongly that most of the things that cause us stress are completely out of our control.

We have no control over the fact that we have too much work to do. We have no control over the fact that customers are yelling at us. We have no control over the fact we got pulled into some meeting. We have no control over the fact that we are late for a meeting and there is traffic. We don't have control over any of those things. BUT, I do believe we have control over how we respond to those things. We always have that.

So, I tell the class that even though we might be in a stressful business, we do have some control over how we respond to situations. I also strongly believe that stress is a habit we have gotten ourselves into under certain situations. We are in the habit of feeling stress when customers start to get upset, when customers start putting demands on us, when management gives us too much work.

We are even in the habit of always assuming the worst and stressing ourselves out. Especially when we are asked to do something we are not comfortable with, like when I ask everybody to pick a team captain. Everybody pointed at somebody else. And the reason that happens is because we are in the habit of assuming the worst. Here is a challenge, here is something we are not comfortable with and it causes us stress. Therefore, we try to get rid of it by not engaging in it.

At this point, I usually tell them, "Just to prove my point, I want to let all of the team captains know something. Your ONLY responsibility today as team captain is to pick who else from your team has to come up here and do role-plays. That's it. That's all you have to do."

Usually the class will laugh at that, and I will see big smiles on the faces of all the team captains, because usually they were forced into it. They didn't want to be team captain, but now they realize it is the best job at the table.

I will point out to the class, *"Now for those of you who don't believe that stress is a habit and don't believe that we always assume the worst, look at what just happened. I never said that the team captains would be involved in role-plays. I simply said that team captains would play a very important part regarding role-plays. Everybody assumed the worst, started pointing around at other people. Here is what I want you to think about. Any stress that any of the team captains felt was 100% self induced; it wasn't based in reality at all. Again, we get in the habit of assuming the worst and stressing ourselves out about it."*

So, going back to the dividing line I mentioned. There is a dividing line, and as a matter of fact, I just put that particular class through it. Imagine the word "exceptional" written on a flip chart and the words "everybody else" written at the bottom of the flip chart, and a little dividing line between them.

EXCEPTIONAL
EVERYBODY ELSE

That dividing line represents some things that truly exceptional performers have, or are in some way different, than everybody else. The exercise of picking team captains is just one of them. One of the quick, easy dividing lines for people who have the potential for being truly exceptional performers is very simple, they are not afraid of failure.

The fear of failure is not something that is on the minds of exceptional performers. They don't see it as failure. They see doing something wrong, and then correcting themselves as an indispensable part of getting better. To them, doing something wrong is not even failure.

They're fine with doing something wrong so that they can improve themselves. This isn't failure, it's development!

When they are faced with a challenge of something they are not to certain about, exceptional performers don't get that stressed out feeling because they are not afraid of failing. They don't run for the hills. They are focused on getting better, and they know that in order to get better they have to take risks and be uncomfortable and simply learn from it.

Now, the truly exceptional performer is not afraid of failure…but they are afraid of something. As a matter of fact, the truly exceptional performer is petrified of it. They are more afraid of this than most of us are afraid of failure. Would you like to try to guess at what that would be?

When I ask a class to guess what the truly exceptional performer is afraid of, usually someone will say, "They are afraid of not being recognized." My response is, "No, they are not afraid of that at all." Someone else will say, "They are afraid of being blamed." And again I will say, "No, they are not afraid of that." Someone will say, "Their spouse." To that I will say they might be afraid of their spouse, but that is not part of the dividing line.

Other people will say things like, "being bored," "success," "having too much work to do," and such. My answer to all of these is no, they are not afraid of that. What the truly exceptional performer is afraid of is mediocrity. That's right, they are actually afraid of being mediocre. Now, a lot of people will say to me you can't be afraid of something like mediocrity. Oh, yes you can! The best performers I have ever met were people who were literally petrified of being mediocre.

I know that they will take chances that most people won't simply because they are afraid of mediocrity. They don't want to be just as good as everybody else, and even if they fail, it's okay because to them it's not failure; it's an indispensable part of actually getting better. I know that when I ask for volunteers in my classes, while most people are sitting around scared to death they might look dumb in front of their friends, the truly exceptional performer is thinking, "What? You mean I'm only as good as everyone else in the room? You mean I'm going to sit here and coast by like everyone else? No way!" And they will volunteer.

Since I just <u>know</u> you want an example of this, here you go.

CHAPTER 7

Wisdom Born of Pain

Yes, I am wise, but it's wisdom born of pain.
Yes I've paid the price, but look how much I've gained.
If I have to, I can do anything.
"I Am Woman" – Helen Reddy

I once had a student ask me, "How do I get ahead of the game?" I told him about Larry.

A few years after a trade book I had written, *The 8 Characteristics of the Awesome Claims Adjuster*, had come out, I was teaching a class in Florida. Ted, a regional manager friend of mine came into my classroom before the class started and said, "Carl I've got a guy just like you described in your book, man. I mean Larry is absolutely unbelievable! He cares about customer service, he has a positive attitude, he takes the initiative on things to get the answer and he knows more after two years than most of my people know after five years. He's incredible!"

I said, "Wow, I would really like to meet this Larry guy." And he said, "You're going to meet him because he is going to be in class today. Would you like me to introduce you?" I said, No, you don't have to introduce me; I'll be able to pick him out. He looked at me rather puzzled and said, "You can just pick him out, you mean just by looking at him?"

"Well no," I said, "Not just by looking at him. You see, truly exceptional performers come in both genders, all educational backgrounds, races and experience levels. None of that means much. But I will be able to pick him out simply because I know there are certain dividing lines between great performers and everybody else." Surprised, he asked, "So do you think you will be able to pick him out by the end of the day?" And I said, "I'll be able to pick him out in the first hour. No problem."

Sure that I was crazy, he said, "I'll bet you 50 bucks you can't do that." And I said, "Okay, I'll bet you $50.00."

You see, that is an easy bet for me, because I know something Ted doesn't know. Truly exceptional performers reveal themselves very quickly; you just have to know what to look for. So I started off that class just as I mentioned before. I asked every team to pick a team captain, and of course everybody started pointing around looking at each other trying to get someone else to be team captain.

Except this one person at a table where I happened to be standing said, "I'll do it. I'll be team captain." He actually raised his hand and volunteered. This caught my attention. Now this doesn't mean he is exceptional, this can just mean he is a goof-off and he just wants a platform. So I had to find out why he wanted to be team captain.

I walked over to the guy and I said, "So, why do you want to be captain?" He thought about it for a second and responded, "Well, my manager is here, my coworkers are here, if I do a really good job, that gives me a chance to shine. I mean, how often do you get that opportunity?" And I said, "Well yes, but what if I call you to the front of the class and make a fool of you? What if you sound silly and do something dumb and you're embarrassed? What if I crack you like an egg, or turn you into Jell-O up there?"

He shrugged his shoulders, and said, "Well, then I will probably learn something I didn't know, and I will be better off for it. **Either way, I'm ahead of the game.**"

I turned to make sure Ted was watching, which he was. I turned back to this guy, stuck out my hand and said, "Glad to have you in class Larry." And Ted said, "Fifty bucks. My wife's going to kill me."

I don't need all day. I don't even need an hour. Heck, I can find an exceptional performer in five minutes. You see, outstanding performers are not afraid of failure. They are afraid of being mediocre.

57

So that night, Ted and I went out for drinks. He paid me $50.00 and I spent $75.00 buying the drinks. So I'm not sure I won overall, but I did prove my point.

The thing about truly exceptional performers is they are not afraid of failure. They are afraid of mediocrity. Because of this, I know in class when I ask for volunteers, I know some of the first people who are going to volunteer are people who don't live in fear that they will fail, they fear being only as good as everybody else. Like I mentioned, they will actually say to themselves, "You mean, I am just going to sit here in class and not volunteer, and not take a risk just like everybody else? I am going to play it safe? I am no better than anybody else in this room?" And that drives them crazy.

The exceptional performers are usually some of the first people that volunteer in class because they don't see making mistakes or looking foolish while trying something new as failure. As a matter of fact, they will think, "You mean the only thing I have to do to distinguish myself from others is volunteer and get up there? That is the only price I am going to pay for getting better? The only price I have to pay for my manager to respect me for having the guts to get up there is having my friends tease me a little? That's it? No problem."

I believe there is a difference between this "Exceptional" person, according to his regional manager, and everyone else. He's not afraid of failure. He's afraid of being only as good as he used to be. And by the way, do you think he is being driven by his ability, or his attitude? That's right. Larry, who impresses the hell out of his regional manager almost constantly, is not doing so because of his ability. His performance is being driven by his attitude. And his attitude is "Doing something wrong and getting better because of it is not failure. It is an indispensible step toward self improvement." I've heard once somewhere that performance is 80% attitude, and 20% ability.

This is one of many dividing lines. I'll bring up a few more as the book progresses. But keep in mind, to an exceptional performer, the only failure is not trying.

Just as a side note, I should tell you that in this particular class, which had Larry in it, I explained to the class what exercise I just put them through and encouraged them to volunteer because I wanted them to stretch out of their comfort zone. I told them how exceptional performers are not afraid of failure.

Well, this one gentleman came up to me after the second break quite incensed. He said to me, "Mr. Van, are you saying that I can't be an exceptional performer just because I don't like doing role-plays? I don't like being in front of people. I get nervous in front of people and I don't like it. I would rather stay at my table. Are you saying I can't be an exceptional performer just because I don't want to do role-plays in front of people? Is that what you're saying?"

My response was, "No, that is not what I am saying. What I am saying is, as long your focus is on protecting yourself rather than improving yourself you have limited your potential. You see, there is a barrier that you have set, over which you will not cross, even if it means you'll get better. Even if it means you can improve yourself, you won't do it because you have set up a barrier and you don't like crossing that barrier. Oh, and by the way, **you** set up the barrier, nobody else did. Oh, and one other thing, you have barriers all over the place. Believe me, that is not the only one."

I continued, "The difference between exceptional performers and everyone else is they have almost no barriers; there is almost nothing they won't do to get better. Their total focus is on getting better and not on whether they look silly in front of their friends. They gain wisdom from the pain."

"If the only price you have to pay to improve" I elaborated, "is to look silly and you are not willing to do it, don't blame anyone but yourself. You are limiting your potential. And by the way, it has almost nothing to do with your ability, and almost everything to do with your attitude. That is what I am saying."

Sure, wish I had some percentages to give him!

CHAPTER 8

The Price of a Memory

The price of a memory,
is the memory of the sorrow it brings.
"Mrs. Potters Lullaby" – Counting Crows

Most employees, like most people in general, live their lives believing that attitude is a function of all the things that happened to them, rather than something that they can affect and change.

Let me ask you, the reader, to ponder a question. If I were to say to you, "Your attitude is probably one of the more important factors of your success in your career, would you agree or disagree?"

Most people would agree, but now let me ask you another question. What have you actively done today to improve your attitude towards your responsibilities in your career, your job satisfaction or anything at all? When I say actively, I mean what have you actually done today; if not today, last week; if not last week, last month? What have you actively done to try to create an improved, more positive attitude in yourself?

Most people, although they will agree attitude is one of the most important factors of their success in their career don't actually do anything to change their attitude. Is attitude something that you can change? Is attitude something you can control? Well, you are going to have to answer that question, and I am going to have to give you some guidelines for what you can do to change your attitude (if you want to).

I believe people have the ability to change their attitudes. The only problem is . . . they don't want to, especially the ones with bad attitudes. Many people who have a poor attitude like their attitude. They believe they are justified in their attitude, even if it is negative.

They believe they are entitled to be angry with the company, annoyed by their supervisors, frustrated with their lack of responsibilities, etc.

And maybe they are. Yet it doesn't hurt anyone except themselves. They will cling to this baggage with all their might because they believe they are entitled to it; that they have earned it.

So, what's wrong with that?

When I lived in Franklin, Tennessee, I was in church listening to a sermon by our pastor, Randy Dunnavant, at Church of the Good Shepherd. Although, I do not remember the exact focus of the sermon, I do remember one important part of it.

Randy was talking about holding grudges and how some people have the ability to hold onto a grudge for an extremely long time. During the sermon, he commented, "Holding a grudge does nothing to the other person. Holding a grudge has no affect whatsoever on the person that you are holding it against. Holding a grudge only has an effect on you. It reminds you of the pain that you went through in order to hold the grudge in the first place. You're paying a price to hold onto that memory"

That was an important comment: it points out that grudges, just like attitudes, are something that we choose to have and, therefore, can choose to alter. But can you choose to have a good attitude? Well, that depends what you're looking for, which I will discuss in the next chapter. However, please keep an open mind that perhaps attitude is something you can control more than you might have thought.

CHAPTER 9

See the World You Make

Ugly ducklings don't turn in to swans,
and glide off down the lake.
Whether your sunglasses are off or on,
you only see the world you make.
"Thing Called Love" – Bonnie Raitt

What is it you are looking for?

Although it might be difficult in book form, I'd like to ask you to do something that I sometimes have my students do. Right now, while you are reading this book, when I tell you to look, I want you to stop reading this page and look around the room for anything that is blue. Anything at all that is blue, or any shade of blue. I would like to see how observant you are.

When you get to the end of this page, stop reading, look around the room, try to observe everything you can that is blue and then look back down at this book and turn the page.

LOOK FOR BLUE NOW . . . THEN TURN THE PAGE

Now, cup your hands around your eyes so that you only see this page. Without looking up from your book, think of everything you just saw . . . that was red. Do not take your eyes of this page. But stop for a moment, before you continue on with the next paragraph and think of anything that you can remember that you just saw that was red.

-PAUSE HERE TO THINK-

Did you find that difficult? Why? Was there any red at all in the room? Could you remember it? Why not? You might think that I tricked you and you will respond by saying, "Well, you told me to look for blue so of course I didn't see red." And you will have underscored my very point.

The point is that people see what they are looking for.

Human beings are pretty simple creatures. We see what we are looking for. There might have been red all around you; there might have been red right in front of you. Why didn't you see it? Because we often overlook what is right in front of us if we are looking for something else hard enough. That is the point.

I can get you to see anything I want! I can get you to see blue, green, or red. I can get you to see triangles, circles, or squares. All I have to do is tell you to look for it, and you will see it. Even to the exclusion of what is right in front of you.

So what exactly is the point again? The point is that your attitude is shaped by what you see. You only see the world you make. You can control what you see by controlling what you are looking for. Therefore, believe it or not, you can choose to have a more positive attitude if you want to!

Have you ever known anybody with a bad attitude? These aren't bad people; they are just seeing what they are looking for. They are not bad in any way, but since they are looking for the bad in things, that is what they see.

You know the type of person I'm talking about. You say to this person, "Hey it's sunny outside" and they'll respond, "No, I don't want to go outside, I'll just get sunburned!"

You say to this person, "Well, maybe it will rain then" and they'll respond, "Oh, I just washed my car, dammit!"

You say to this person, "Hey, I am going to give you a big fat raise" and the person will respond, "No . . . that's more taxes . . . I don't want it."

Is this a bad person? No, this person is just seeing what he is looking for and that is all. The funny thing is, it is what this person is looking for, whether positive or negative,

67

that will affect his success and his career more than any other skill, talent, or technique that his masters.

Can it be changed? Yes, but we still need to do a little more homework. I need to tell you about The Rochelle Roy Response.

PART 2

Attitude is Job Satisfaction

CHAPTER 10

A Smile for Everyone

I've got a smile, for everyone I meet.
As long as you don't try draggin' my bay,
Or dropping a bomb on my street.
"Middle of the Road" – Pretenders

The Rochelle Roy Response is what I call the reaction I always look for in potential hires. I would like to take a minute and tell you what happened one day to me and Rochelle Roy. Rochelle was an employee of mine when I was a manager. I considered her an outstanding employee. I really didn't know why; all I knew was that I could trust her and she would always do a good job.

Rochelle was pleasant, friendly, helpful, and generally a very responsible employee. Even though she had a tough job, she enjoyed the interaction with her coworkers and customers. She smiled when she met someone new, which made her very attractive. She was the mother of two boys, and seemed to be able to handle chaos evenhandedly.

One day I entered the break room and I saw Rochelle reading her company manual. Just as I walked in, I heard somebody say, "Shelly, it's just not fair that Carl gives you all this extra work to do. He's always giving you extra projects, expecting you to make extra efforts, and it's just not fair. He should spread the work around, and not make you carry such a load. You should say something to him."

Now, I was ready to spout out my righteous indignation by saying something along the lines of, "Well I am the manager here, and I can do whatever the heck I want to… " or whatever I was going to say. But before I could spit that out, Rochelle stopped reading, looked up at this person and said, "I know Carl gives me a lot of extra work to do. He must think highly of me and trust me quite a bit to do that. And when people think highly of me, I work hard not to let them down." Then she resumed reading her manual.

Of course, I resisted the urge to drop to my knees like Wayne and Garth and cry out, "I'm not worthy, I'm not worthy," because that was a pretty good response, don't you think? As a matter of fact, it was an outstanding response. Somehow, Rochelle recognized that all of the extra work I gave her was my outward expression that I believed in her more than anybody else.

Somehow, Rochelle recognized that I must have trusted her highly or else I wouldn't have given her extra work.

I wouldn't have placed my faith in her for all to see. Somehow, amongst all of the work, Rochelle could recognize this opportunity when she saw it.

The most obvious display of someone with a positive attitude is when that person can recognize opportunity when they see it. There is a saying, "The trouble with opportunity is that it is disguised as hard work." And that's true; that's a big problem with opportunity.

Bear in mind, Rochelle was not someone who walked around the office, glad that she got five hours of work dumped on her on a Friday at 4:30 pm. She had her days when the work piled up, and she had her days when dealing with customers would get frustrating. But somehow, she recognized that the extra work she was being asked to do was an opportunity. Somewhere in all that work was an opportunity that no one else got, the opportunity to prove that she could do it when maybe no one else could. The opportunity to prove my faith in her wasn't misplaced.

How about that person who made the comment to Rochelle? Was she trying to help Rochelle, or bring her down? Probably bring her down. You know, there are people (and these are not bad people either), that honestly believe the only way they can succeed is to bring everyone else around them down. They walk around dropping bombs on people's streets. They are not trying to be mean, they simply have no idea of how to achieve without bringing other people down.

Rochelle saw that comment for what it was — an attempt to discourage her positive attitude, and she would have nothing of it. She saw that my extra demands on her were my outward expression that I trusted and thought more of her than anyone else. She was not about to throw away a hard earned opportunity like that.

Now, let me tell you about what I call my own personal Non-Rochelle Roy Response. Because Rochelle's response was a whole lot better than my response about three weeks earlier.

Tom Higgins was my boss. He was the one who had promoted me several times In order for me to reach my manager position at the time, so I really felt I owed him a lot. I respected him. He was organized, hard working, and really expected quite a bit out of the people around him.

Tom had light brownish reddish hair, and a full brownish reddish mustache which was always very well groomed (better than his hair). He had these wide wire rim glasses that he adjusted on his face constantly when he talked, that had a way of telling you, "This is important. Pay attention."

Tom was very accepting of mistakes, as long as you learned from them. Whenever someone felt bad about making a mistake, he would always say, "Hey, nobody's perfect. In fact, there was only one perfect person who ever lived, and they crucified him!" He was very personal, but quite direct in his delivery of feedback. Especially to me (sniff)!

I was in Tom's office, and I was bitching, whining, and complaining like you wouldn't believe. I was saying things like, "The other managers wanted me to do this, and HR asked me to do that, and that took all day Saturday, and now I have to do this traveling, and blah, blah, blah."

I was complaining, bitching, whining, and crying for five, six, maybe seven minutes or so. I bitched and complained, and then bitched some more (I figured I was bound to get a company car out of this or something). But the whole time I was complaining, Tom was just staring at me, waiting for me to finish.

Finally, after about six, seven minutes or so, I ran myself down and stopped. Tom looked at me for a few seconds and said, "Carl, are you finished?" And I said, "Yeah, I'm finished." And he said, "Good, because I want to remind you of something." And I said, "Yeah… what?"

He said as he adjusted his glasses, "Carl, you asked for this job, remember? You sat here . . . in this office . . . and went into detail about how tough this job was going to be and why you were the only person I should select.

Carl, you practically begged me for this job. 22 people applied for this job, Carl, and you got it. I saw something in you I didn't see in anybody else. Maybe I was right, and maybe I was wrong, but here's your chance to prove it either way."

Slumping down in my chair, I listened as he continued, "If you want an easy job, go to McDonald's; a little buzzer goes off when the fries have to come out. If that's what you want no hard feelings. Go! But before you leave my office, Carl, let me remind you of something. You got something 21 other people didn't get. You got the <u>chance</u> to prove you could do this job. No one else even got the chance. So do what you want to do."

Now, this wasn't a "Win one for the Gipper" speech, this was a "Get your ass out of my office because you begged me for this job," speech. And guess what? Tom was right! I did beg him for that job. I sat in his office for four hours interviewing for that promotion, telling him how tough it was going to be and how no one else could do it. I wanted the title, I wanted the respect, I wanted the challenge, and I sure as hell wanted the money. Yet, once I got the job, all I could see was the hard work. All I could see were the demands and the tough things I had to do. I knew it was a tough job, which was why I asked for it in the first place. I just couldn't see the opportunity anymore; all I could see was the hard work.

Somehow Tom, my boss, recognized that all of the extra hard work I was going to have to do was my opportunity to prove that he was right for hiring me in the first place. That all of that hard work was my opportunity to show I was the right person for the job. The hard work was the challenge that I wanted, and would let me experience the satisfaction I would feel from knowing I could do a difficult job that not many people could do.

Somehow, Rochelle, my own employee, recognized that all of the extra work I was giving her was my outward expression that I believed in her, and the hard work was her opportunity to prove me right. Somehow, I was the only one in this mix not getting it.

My attitude had gotten turned around and I found myself looking for the wrong things. It wasn't entirely my fault, I simply hadn't been trained. Trained in what? Trained in how to recognize opportunity when it is there. To show you what I mean I must tell you the story of the "Acres of Diamonds."

CHAPTER 11

Diamonds

People say she's crazy; she's got
diamonds on the souls of her shoes.
Well, that's one way to lose these walking blues.
"Diamonds on the Souls of Her Shoes" – Paul Simon

"Acres of Diamonds" is a story written by Russell Conwell. I first heard about the "Acres of Diamonds" in a book called *The Psychology of Achievement* by Brian Tracy. Mr. Tracy does an outstanding job paraphrasing the story, and I will try to do the same.

"Acres of Diamonds" is a short story about an old African farmer at the turn of the century. He's doing quite well on his farm. However, one day he hears about people discovering diamond mines and becoming fabulously wealthy. So he sells his land, sells his tools, sells all of his animals and heads off into Africa in search of diamond mines.

Well, 12, 13, 15 years later, broke, destitute and alone, he throws himself into the ocean and drowns. Meanwhile back on his farm, the new farmer is watering down his donkey in a stream. He looks down and he sees a rock; a rock that reflects light in a remarkable way.

He picks up the rock and takes it into town, and someone who knew what it was says, "Well, this is a diamond." And the farmer says, "It doesn't look like a diamond."

The man replies, "Well no, it doesn't look like a diamond. You have to cut it, clean it, and shine it, but it's a diamond. Can you take me back to where you found it?" So the farmer took the man back to his farm.

They went back to the farmer's land, and the new farmer looked down on his land and saw another rock. He picked it up and saw that it also was a diamond. Then he saw another rock, and that was a diamond. Again he found another rock, and that was a diamond. And lo and behold, he looks up, and he finds that he is literally standing on acres of diamonds.

Now the moral of the story isn't that *if you want something you have to look under your own two feet*. The moral of the story is, *if you are going to look for something, you'd better know what it's going to look like when you find it*. This goes back to the old saying that the trouble with opportunity is that it is disguised as hard work.

Most of us want opportunity. We want a job that's challenging and to be praised when it is done well.

Unfortunately, sometimes we don't see that we have that very job we were looking for, simply because we don't know how to recognize it when we find it.

It is hard to imagine, but sometimes the challenges and opportunities you desire most may well be what you have in your hands. If so, you may be a little bit like Mike Rhoda.

CHAPTER 12

Wanting What You've Got

*It's not getting what you want,
It's wanting what you've got.*
"Soak up the Sun" – Sheryl Crow

I had a situation. It was the Mike Rhoda situation.

As a manager in a claims office (admission #2), I once had an employee named Mike Rhoda. I considered Mike to be an excellent employee; intelligent, hardworking, and conscientious.

As one can imagine, when you work in the claims business a while and have people trying to exaggerate their claims on a regular basis, you can get a little skeptical.

I remember Mike's wife coming up to me at a party one time saying "Carl, I want my husband back. He's been a claims employee for six months and he doesn't believe anything anybody tells him anymore." I responded with

"Why, what happened?" She said "We had friends over the other night. When they told us they had gone on a cruise, Mike asked them if they had photos to prove it."

Anyway, one day Mike came up to me and we had the following conversation:

Rhoda:	*You know Carl, being a claims employee is not what I want.*
Van:	*What is it that you want?*
Rhoda:	*I want a job where I have responsibility.*
Van:	*Responsibility? You practically hold people's lives in your hands, while you're handling their claim.*
Rhoda:	*Well, I want a job where I have authority.*
Van:	*Authority? You've got authority. You can write a ten thousand dollar check without blinking. How many of your friends can pay out ten thousand dollars of their company's money without needing someone else's approval?*
Rhoda:	*Well, I want a job where I can help people.*
Van:	*Help people? These people are in desperate need of help.*
Rhoda:	*No, they just whine, and cry, and bitch.*
Van:	*Well Mike . . . what do people DO when they need help? What does a job like that **look** like?*
Rhoda:	(Shrugs)

Van: *Yes, Mike, you have a difficult job. You have to deal with heavy workloads. You have to deal with upset customers. You have to deal with internal procedures that get in the way. You have to deal with vendors, phone calls, interruptions. Yes, yes. You have a difficult job. But that's why we hired <u>you</u>. Plenty of people applied for this job, but you're the one we hired. If this was an easy job, we wouldn't need talented people. We'd just hire less talented people and pay them less.*

Just about then I got off my soapbox and tried to help Mike see that the very things he wanted, he already had. He just couldn't recognize them.

I've seen people leave their industry simply because they did not recognize they already had the very thing that they were seeking, ordinary things. The first step in becoming an exceptional performer is the desire to improve. From that point on, it is focusing on recognizing opportunities when they are there and being able to see them through all the hard work. It's not easy, but it's not impossible.

CHAPTER 13

Watch Out!

Watch out! You might get what you're after.
"Burning Down the House" – Talking Heads

I knew a guy who worked at another company. His name was Craig, and was an auto appraiser, writing estimates on cars. He used to hand write the estimates. He used to have to inspect the cars, photograph the damage, and he used to have to write up the cost of the repairs by looking up the part prices in something called a Mitchell Manual. Then he would calculate the hours of repair by considering the "overlap" of operations and "included operations" of certain parts. It took a lot of training and a lot of practice.

Then one day, he and his coworkers heard about this system called Auto-Tech. It was this great new automatic system that he thought would just be the most fantastic thing in the world. It was a system where all he would have to do is mark the damaged parts on a piece of paper, input the information into a processer, and out would come an estimate complete with part prices, labor times, overlap operations, etc. It was going to make their lives so fantastic. At the time, he could write only four large estimates a day, and this was going to make their life so much easier.

So, they asked management for the system over and over again and management just wouldn't go for it. The other appraisers asked him to help pitch the idea to upper management, so he did.

He did a lot of research and came back with a proposal to upper management on this new system; on how it was going to decrease errors, increase production, and raise overall quality.

Well, after six months of pushing and pushing, they finally got the system. And you know what? It was everything they dreamed of. It was fantastic. It took a lot less time to complete an estimate and it did a tremendous amount of the work for them. It actually made their lives easier.

Of course the first thing that happened is that management increased the standard for how many estimates they had to write in a day. Instead of four, now they had to write five. Well, he was the one who said productivity would go up, right?

The next thing they did was to lower the limit for the number of errors on their estimates. Well, he was the one who said accuracy would increase, wasn't he?

But, you know what? It still made their lives easier. They still didn't need to kill themselves arguing with body shops over the right parts, or the parts prices, or have to look up things nearly as often in the Mitchell Manual.

So, he got what he asked for. He got an easier job. There is no doubt about it. This job was actually easier now. And he got lots of "hero cookies" and pats on the back from other appraisers because they knew it was he who helped push through this program. He was definitely the star of the show at the time.

Then a few months later, he was getting his performance review. As he walked into the room with his manger Peter, the human resources manager, Julie was sitting in the room already. Julie was about 25 years old but looked about 14. She was quiet, polite, but always looked scared that someone might yell at her. She wore nothing but dresses, usually with patterns that featured some kind of fruit. When she got really nervous, she would make a noise that fell between a hiccup and a sneeze. Sort of like a "snnn-ick." And Craig thought, "Oh, this is good. I must be getting a new company car or something."

Well, he sat down and Peter gave him his performance review telling him he did really well in all areas and they were very happy with his performance. And at the end, he said, "But, you know what Craig, we can't give you a raise." And so Craig said, "You can't give me a raise? Why can't you give me a raise? You're telling me I did such a great job, plus I helped push through the Auto-Tech system." And Peter said, "Yeah, well that's the issue at hand Craig, that Auto-Tech system. That's why Julie from HR is here."

Julie said, "Well Craig, we want to let you know that we have had to downgrade your position. You were at a 20, but now you are at a 16. We had to downgrade it and now you are at the top of the pay scale and we can't give you a raise." Of course Craig said, "Downgrade my position? How could you downgrade my position?" And she said, "Well Craig, we have this new Auto-Tech system now, and the appraisal process isn't nearly as complicated as it used to be."

Getting irritated, Craig said "I just know you're joking!" She continued, "I mean before, you used to have to know all about the cars, the parts, the pricing and such, snnn-ick! Now with this new system, all we have to do is hire people who can look at a car and identify the part and the Auto-Tech system does the rest, snnn-ick! So the job isn't nearly as complicated as it used to be, and we have downgraded the position from a 20 to a 16 and now you're at the top of the pay scale, snnnnnnnnnn-ick."

So, sitting there stunned, Craig realized he had gotten exactly what he had asked for. He'd asked for an easier job and he got it.

What's the moral of that story? Watch out! You might get what you're after. And he got it. So the point is I suppose that every once in a while, when we as employees are running around complaining about how hard our job is and how difficult it is and how demanding it is, to remember something. To remember, yes, it's true that we have a difficult job, but then again that's why we got the job. If it was an easy job, anyone could do it. And that if we continue to push to make our job easier, we might just make our job so easy that no one needs us.

Most people have no idea how to change their attitude even if they want to. To give you an example of how hard it can be, and to give you hope that if Bob can do it, anyone can, I will share the saga of Bob.

MIKESHAPIRO

CHAPTER 14

Bad Moon Rising

I see the bad moon arising, I see trouble on the way.
I see earthquakes and lightning, I see bad times today.
"Bad Moon Rising" – Credence Clearwater Revival

The saga of Bob starts back when I was a new manager. Before I had the opportunity to meet the people I would be managing, Ryan, my predecessor, took me aside and gave me the run-down on everyone I would be managing.

Ryan was great and the ultimate team player. He never cared about getting credit or glory. He only cared about results for the office as a whole. Ryan was young for his position, thin, and a fast talker. In my entire career, he is the only one of my predecessors who took the time necessary to bring me up to speed on the staff instead of just the duties.

Ryan told me things like, "Susan is a hard worker. She is stubborn, but she is a valuable asset because she follows the rules. Use her to help carry out procedures." Great advice.

He said other things like, "Dan is creative and a problem solver. He doesn't mind change, but he can get bored very easily. Make sure you keep him challenged with new opportunities." More great advice.

During the end of this briefing, he said something to me that I will never forget. He said, "Now, Good Ole Bob here, he is very knowledgeable. He's very technically sound; you just have to watch out because he has a bad attitude."

During the conversation, Ryan went into detail about the bad attitude Bob displayed at meetings and around the office, and how many times in his past performance reviews Bob had been told that he needed to improve. I didn't think too much of it at the time until it hit home.

At our first office meeting, I found that this office had a particular routine.

Someone would bring up something new; some kind of change she would like to see, and then everyone would all wait for good ole Bob to say something nasty or negative about it. He would, of course, and then we would continue to talk about it to see if we could work something out. It was like a little dance that we'd all do in giving Bob his opportunity to get it out and move on with business.

It didn't take me too long until I realized that this was a very negative influence. As a matter of fact, we showed Bob more respect, and gave him more time than just about anybody else because we all knew it was coming. In order to ease the pain of it happening, we all just waited for it to happen and then continued on. The bad side of this was often he would convert someone to his side with his negative thinking before anybody really got any time to consider what we were trying to do.

Not only that, but then I noticed that during the day, Bob would spend time in the break room, chatting with other people, always promoting his negativism, which of course can be contagious. What Ryan told me was true, Bob was an excellent technician. He did his job according to his job responsibilities very well. Unfortunately, I spent a lot of time trying to clean up issues that had been twisted around by Bob. It didn't take too long until I realized that I had to do something about this problem.

At first I thought, I can sit down with Bob and go through all the things he needs to change and how it will help him in his career if he does make a change in his attitude. Then, I had a chance to read his past five performance reviews and realized that he's been told this for many, many years. In fact, he has admitted many times that he is always being told that he needs to change his attitude, and he'll even agree that that is something he needs to do in order to get promoted. Yet he would never actually change anything.

Then, I thought well, maybe I should give him some extra responsibilities and have him be responsible for leading a project. Yes, that would work. Put him in charge of fixings the things he says need fixing. I thought this was a perfect idea until Brad Baumann, a friend and coworker of mine pointed out that all that would do was show everyone in the office that the way you get rewarded with extra responsibilities is to bitch and complain about everything. That will send exactly the wrong message.

So I really didn't know what I was going to do until one day I decided I couldn't take it anymore, and I decided to give myself a gift. I decided to give myself a present; I decided then and there that in 30 days I was not going to have this problem anymore. In 30 days, this issue would be over. Either I would fire Bob, or I would fix him. One of the two was absolutely going to happen in 30 days. After that date, I thought to myself, I would not have this problem anymore.

Oh, and since I really didn't have any idea on how to fix Bob, I subconsciously decided that I was going to fire him. Being an ex-auditor, I knew that would be very easy to do. No matter how good someone's work was, I could always find something wrong and blow it up into a big deal. That's what auditors do; didn't you know that?

So this really wouldn't be a problem at all. I mentally placed a big fat red "x" on the back of Bob's head, and I set my sights.

I knew it would take me the whole 30 days to do it, and I hunkered down to organize my action plan. I was going to get rid of this piece of evil that was a barrier to office attitude Nirvana. This bad seed was going down, and I was convinced firing Bob was the only realistic option . . . until that night.

That night something amazing happened. I happened to be watching an episode of "All in the Family." Meathead and Gloria were going off to protest something at a state office or something like that, and this was clearly irritating Archie. Meathead and Archie were arguing about it for a few minutes when Archie finally says to Meathead, "Look, if you don't like this country why don't you just get the hell out!"

When I heard that, I jumped up and said, "Yeah, Bob, if you don't like it in my office and it's so bad, then why don't you get the hell out of my office!" And I was cheering Archie on. I was cheering him on until Meathead said something that absolutely blew me away. Meathead responds to Archie, "Archie, I love this country, that's why I complain when I see something wrong."

That comment surprised me because I realized that Meathead wasn't complaining for complaining sake, he was actually trying to change something. He was trying to change what was happening into something better. It hit me right then and there, that people who complain and bitch and always point out the negative may not be bad people.

They may honestly believe that in order to help, they must point out all of the pitfalls. In their minds, to be helpful, they have to warn people of the things that could happen or why things may not work. They're trying to help us avoid all of the death, disease and destruction if something doesn't work out. They might not be bad people; <u>they are just seeing what they are looking for!</u>

That evening I decided I wasn't going to give up on Bob just yet. I decided to give Bob the benefit of the doubt and to see what I could do to actually affect change. I reread his performance reviews and realized something interesting. Although every single manager Bob ever had pointed out in detail that he needed to change his attitude in order for him to avoid being fired or receive promotions, they left out the most important thing. They left out <u>how</u> he was supposed to change.

How would Bob go about changing his attitude? No one had given him any instruction or any training whatsoever on how to actually do this. I realized that for five years Bob had been asked to do something he had no training in and no instruction on; he was just told to do it. I decided I was going to help Bob make that change. Well at least for the next 29 days I'd help him. Now I was faced with the same problem everyone else had: how do I get Bob to change?

I have found there's a key to getting people to change. Keep in mind, most people like their attitude. They cling to it. They believe that they deserve it and that they are entitled to it, so they don't want to let it go. We all know that the only way to get someone to change is if they want to change.

There's an old joke my mother once told me that goes like this (bear in mind I didn't say it was a funny joke): How many psychiatrists does it take to change a light bulb? The answer is, it only takes one, but the light bulb has to really want to change.

I told you it wasn't funny. Nevertheless, it points out something important. The only way to get Bob to change is getting him to want to change. Until he wanted to, it was pointless. So that became my number one focus. How will I get Bob to want to change?

Well, I could do what all the other managers in the past had done and threaten him with losing his job, and that would probably work for a short period of time until he had been removed from written warning long enough to go back to his old ways.

Or, I could hold out a carrot in front of him and offer promotions and big raises if he changed his attitude, which never worked well before either. Somehow I was going to have to come up with something different. And I really didn't know what that was going to be until I read a fascinating article about a restaurant that changed the answer to the most infamous question in dining history: "Saved room for dessert?"

CHAPTER 15

Mmm, Mmm

Mmm mmm mmm mmm. Mnmm mmm mmm mmm.
"Mmm Mmm Mmm Mmm" – Crash Test Dummies

"Saved room for desert?" Have you ever heard this question? The article I mentioned was written about a restaurant that had a very high percentage of people ordering dessert after their meals (and no, Oprah, I don't remember what it was called!). As everyone knows, the percentage of people ordering dessert after a meal is very low. About 10% would be a good guess. After you have had a nice big meal and the waiter comes over to you and says, "Did you save room for dessert?" Your response probably is, "No." But this restaurant had a very high percentage of people ordering dessert; somewhere around 80% if I can remember correctly. What was it that this restaurant did that all the other restaurants didn't do?

My first thought was, maybe they just didn't feed their customers very much. Maybe the initial portions were really small and they were still hungry. But it turned out that that wasn't the case; their portions were just as big as other restaurant's portions.

The article mentioned that normally a waiter will come over and ask, "Did you save room for dessert?" and most people's response is, "No." Only 10% will say yes. But if a restaurant wants to increase the chance of you ordering dessert, what might they do?

One thing they could do is come over and describe the dessert, tell you what it is, how it's made, etc., and that has a positive effect. It has a positive effect because instead of only imagining there was some mystery dessert out there, you now have the ability to focus on one, such as chocolate mousse or cheesecake. And the better the description of how it is made and prepared and served, the more appetizing it becomes, because now you have to rely less on your imagination. This process does work well and does increase people ordering dessert a couple of percentage points, maybe to 14% or 15%.

Another thing a restaurant could do is to give you a list that describes the desserts. That works well too because now you are actually reading them and getting images in your mind as you are reading them. And this makes you have a connection between the dessert itself and the enjoyment you will receive. This is even more effective than just describing it; however it still relies on your imagining the reward. But, it does push the percentage up to a good 19% or 20%.

Another thing a restaurant can do is to show you a picture of the desserts. This works very well in increasing the percentage another few points. Now there is a stronger connection between the dessert and your imagining what would taste like. The reward becomes more real, but once again it is only a few more percentage points effective, because it still relies on you imagining what it would taste like and the pleasure that you will receive. Let's guess it goes up to 21% or 22%.

In some restaurants (and you know which ones they are), they actually come around with a tray of desserts and point them out to you, describing each one in detail and using all of the techniques that all the other restaurants used except they put that dessert right in front of you. And this works best of all.

This also brings it up a few more percentage points, maybe 25%, heck maybe 30%. Those who have it right in front of their face will order dessert, because it strengthens the bond between imagination and enjoyment. Unfortunately, it still relies on that old tool of getting you to imagine how much you will enjoy it in order to get you motivated to buy it.

Well, 25% to 30% is much better than 10%, but remember, this restaurant I had read about had 80%. How? Simple, they did not rely on what I call the "Imagine This" motivational technique.

Getting people to imagine their reward or to imagine their pain in order to motivate them, in my opinion is not all that effective. Even though we have good imaginations, it is still not real to us.

Take two different people and tell one person to imagine what he would do if they did not have a job right now. Ask him to imagine he was immediately fired, right this moment, and watch him calmly go through describing the opportunities and the choices he would have, and how he would respond.

Now, take the other individual and tell her that she is actually fired, and watch the sheer panic go through her. She is not just imagining it, she is actually experiencing it. Watch her change into another person as the reality of everything that will happen hits her. Watch her become motivated to do whatever it takes to stop this from happening. Or, even if she didn't like her job and were considering leaving it anyway but just never had the time to update her résumé, watch how motivated she becomes now to go look for a better job.

In my opinion, this is an opportunity for improvement for management in the United States: the practice of getting people to imagine either their rewards or their penalties before they have experienced it. How will you ever motivate someone by trying to get him to imagine his reward, before he has experienced it? This is the only tool we have of course, so we use it even though it is not very effective.

I was about to use this same, ineffective tool myself with good ole Bob, until I read this article about a restaurant, and it changed my mind about the limited tools we have at our disposal.

Hopefully you are yelling at this book saying, "So, tell us! What the hell did they do, Carl?"

Okay, okay, don't get in a huff. I'll tell you.

This restaurant did something much more effective than asking someone to use the "Imagine This" technique. They didn't just bring out the dessert; they brought out a tray of only one tiny bite of each of their desserts. Instead of asking customers if they wanted to try it, they simply walked up with the tray, bent down, put the tray in front of the customer and said, "Which one would you like to try?"

Admit it. You, me, and everyone who reads this book all know that no matter how full we are, we can always push in one little piece of cheesecake. There's always room for a little tiny piece of chocolate torte no matter how full we are.

Come on, 'fess up. No matter how full you are, when offered a tiny treat, for free, something's going in!

Guess what would happen when they asked their customers this? Virtually every customer would try at least one little bite. And then, something amazing would happen; they tasted it. It was real; it wasn't imaginary anymore. They would actually taste it; it was in their mouth and it tasted good. They liked it.

What this restaurant found was that there were a very high percentage of people that would now order dessert. It also found that virtually everyone who ordered a dessert ordered the very thing they tasted. That's the way the restaurant knew that there was a high correlation between what people tasted, and what they ordered.

My revelation: If you want someone to really want something, you've got to give them a taste of it.

This was a real motivational force and I decided to use it. If a restaurant could get people to order dessert when they are not hungry simply because they can make that taste real for them, maybe I could do this for Bob. I now had some goals.

The first one was I had to get Bob to want to change; the second was I had to teach him how. I outlined what I needed to do, and I came up with this:

STRATEGY TO GET BOB TO CHANGE:

1. Get him to want to change.
   Find out what he desires.
   Set an expectation so that he can achieve his desires.
   Give him a taste.

2. Teach him how to change.
   Show him he will see what he is looking for.
   Change what he is looking for.

Should be a piece of cake right? Mmm, mmm, mmm, mmm.

CHAPTER 16

Plant a Seed

Plant a seed, plant a flower, plant a rose.
You can plant any one of those.
Keep planting to find out which one grows.
It's a secret no one knows.

"Mmm Bop" – Hansen

Now I needed to plant a seed. I had my strategy.

STRATEGY TO GET BOB TO CHANGE:

1. Get him to want to change.
>   Find out what he desires.
>   Set an expectation so that he can achieve his desires.
>   Give him a taste.

2. Teach him how to change.
>   Show him he will see what he is looking for.
>   Change what he is looking for.

80% of Bob's job satisfaction is his attitude. Change that, and we're home free.

I called Bob into my office and had him sit down. Of course he was a little nervous because most people don't get called into the boss's office unless they are in trouble, but he was relatively calm anyway.

I sat down on the same side of the desk with Bob and I started to talk to him. I wanted to find out the types of things that he wanted and what motivated him. This information didn't come easy, but after 20, maybe 30 minutes or so I found out something very interesting about Bob. Bob was not a bad person. He was absolutely just seeing what he was looking for. He had no way to look for the positive; all he knew how to do was look for the negative.

I found out that what Bob wanted was what everybody wanted. He wanted to be respected for his knowledge, be revered for his ability to do his job; he wanted to be seen as an authority figure in the office, someone people would come to for advice. I saw very little difference in Bob than most of my employees.

However, there is an old saying that goes like this:

There is very little difference between people, but that little difference can make a big difference. The little difference is attitude, and the big difference is whether it is positive or negative.

I now had some advantages that perhaps the previous managers did not have. I now knew that I had to get Bob to want to change, and that I had to give him a taste of what it would be like if he did. I also had to teach him how to do it. I had to give him a process that he could follow. In short, I had to train Bob by giving him a little taste of reality.

Taste of Reality

As sneaky as it might be, this was my approach. About a week after the discussion where I found out about Bob's desire to be respected and valued, I called Bob into my office and once again we had an informal chat. When I felt the time was right, and Bob was somewhat at ease, I said the following to Bob:

"Bob, I just want to thank you and congratulate you for everything you have done. I asked you to make a change in your attitude, and you've done a remarkable job. You have absolutely been a positive influence in the office, and it is returning some great results. People are coming to me now and saying how they were surprised that you really did know so much, and that they wanted you on their teams for their projects. People respect you and they clearly understand how much you really do know. You've made my job easier by being a positive influence in the office and

I want to congratulate you on it. I want to admit to you that many people didn't think you could do it. A lot of people had you down and out for the count; that you didn't have what it takes to make a change. And you've proven every single one of them wrong. You've risen above everybody's expectations, Great job."

Now after I said this to him, he looked rather puzzled, because he knew that he didn't make any change at all. That was okay for the time being. I then asked him an important question. I said to Bob, "Well, how does it feel to get all that feedback?" And Bob said, "Well, it feels pretty good. I'm not sure I deserve it, but it sure feels nice. No one has ever said that to me before; it feels really good."

I paused for a moment or two, and then I said to Bob, "Well, that's good, because that's the feedback I am going to give you when you turn your attitude around"

WHAM! Bob looked like he had just been body slammed. I continued, "That's what I'm going to tell you when you change your attitude in the direction as I've asked you to do. If you like that taste, there is much more coming."

Now you, the reader, might feel that I tricked Bob, and in a way I admit I did. I suppose it was a little sneaky but I gave Bob a taste. Even though he knew he didn't deserve it, he still got a taste of something he had never been given before. He needed to taste that positive feedback; that he was succeeding in the office. And guess what?

He liked it! In fact, he wanted more. And I could see those thoughts running through his mind about how good that tasted and how badly he wanted some more.

He then asked me a question; it was the most important question on his road to recovery. He sat there for a few minutes, gave me a smirk like he knew he had just been bluffed out of a winning hand in poker, tilted his head, sighed heavily and asked, "Okay. What do I have to do?"

Ah, those beautiful words. "What do I have to do?" Right then, when he asked that question, I knew I had something. He was asking what he would have to do to change. I'd given Bob a taste of what he wanted and I got something in return. What I got was a clear indication that Bob wanted to change. He now wanted to change because he had tasted something he liked and he wanted more.

What most managers would have done was to say, "If you change your attitude, here is what you will get." But that's the old "Imagine This" technique.

Step one was done. I had found out what Bob desired. I had given him a reasonable expectation that he could achieve just by making the change. I had given him a taste, and it tasted good. I knew right then and there I had achieved my first objective with Bob. And now came the easy part. Now all I had to do was teach him how he could change and what to look for.

CHAPTER 17

Give a Whistle

If life seems jolly rotten,
then there's something you've forgotten…
When you're chewing on life's gristle,
don't grumble, give a whistle!
"Always Look on the Bright Side of Life" – Monty Python

When I first moved to Nashville, my wife told me, "Carl, you're going to love living in the south." "Why is that" I asked. "Because" she said, "in the south, you can say any nasty thing you want to about anyone, as long as right afterwards; you say 'Bless his heart.'"

Wow, really? What a great tool. And it worked. Here, check it out:

That boy is dumb as a box of hammers…Bless his heart!

And if it was really bad, you had to throw in the word "little." Here, look:

That girl is as homely as a mud fence…Bless her little heart!

Isn't that great? Nice tool to have, huh?

Let's go back to Bob. My personal motto was that you will see what you are looking for; therefore, look for what you hope to see. I tried to put this into play with Bob. What I said to Bob was, "Bob, here's what I want you to do. The next time we are in an office meeting and someone says something about any type of change, what will happen?" Bob responded, "I will find something bad about it."

"Right," I said. "So, here's what I want you to do. When somebody says something is going to happen, instead of that thing happening, I want you to imagine that the opposite will happen. I want you to imagine that whatever circumstance someone mentions, whatever project is brought up, or whatever event has happened, do the best you can to imagine that the opposite happened.

Bob rebutted, "What good will that do, then I'll just see the bad in that." "Yes," I agreed, "but when you automatically think of the negative of that alternate event, then the opposite of that negative will be the positive of the real event."

Bob was looking at me kind of like you are probably looking at this book right now, with a big puzzled look on your face trying to make sense of what I just said. But I have to hand it to Bob, bless his heart, he did his best.

At the next office meeting, we were informed that we were closing down an office near us, and all of that office's work was coming to us. Every bit of work was now going to be handed down to us with the same amount of staff that we currently had. Yes, we would gradually be able to increase our staff, but in the meantime we would all have to handle the extra work. As soon as that announcement was made, everybody (including me) stopped and looked down at the end of the table at Bob. We were all thinking, "This is going to be a good one."

Bob sat there, and before he could say anything, I saw him trying to do what I asked him to do. He sat there rolling his eyes across the top of this eye sockets with this head bobbing up and down like one of those little dogs in the back of a car window, trying to think of what it was I had asked him to do. I could see his lips moving, and I could see his brain thinking, "Okay, let's see, if that's what's happening...the opposite is...that's the negative...hmm, wait...the opposite of that..."

And after about 10 seconds, with his head shaking and saliva drooling out of the corner of his mouth, Bob blurted out, "Well, at least it's job security!"

WHAM! Everybody in the office meeting was stunned. Including, ME. We all turned our heads, looked at Bob, and we were all thinking, "WHAT? That came out of Bob?" Nobody could believe it; Bob had something positive to say and no one knew how it happened. What Bob did was exactly what I asked him to do. (See Figure 20.1)

Figure 17.1

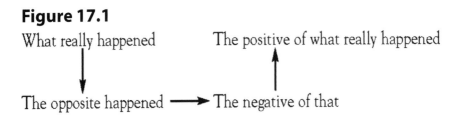

What really happened   The positive of what really happened

The opposite happened ⟶ The negative of that

What I asked Bob to do was for anything that came up, to think of the opposite. So when we were told that the other office was shutting down and the work was coming to us, what does that mean? The real event is that we are going to have to do a lot more work. What I asked Bob to do was imagine the opposite of that event. The opposite of more work is less work. (See Figure 20.2)

Then I asked Bob to come up with the immediate negative of that alternate event. What is the negative of having less work? Well, layoffs.

Once Bob thought of layoffs, I asked him for one more step. I told him that whatever negative he thought of that came out of the alternate event, the opposite of that would be the positive of the real event. And what is the opposite of layoffs? Job security.

Figure 17.2

Situation:

Nearby office is shutting down, and the work is coming to us.

It took him a while, it took a couple seconds of his head bobbing up and down along with some minor drooling, but he somehow got from more work coming into the office to job security. It didn't come easy, but at least he had a process to follow now that he didn't have before.

The first time it took Bob maybe 10 seconds with saliva coming out as he blurted out "job security." After a couple of weeks he stopped slobbering. After a few more weeks, I couldn't see his lips move anymore. After even a few more weeks, I didn't even see him roll his eyes and bob his head anymore. He could get from the event happening, to the positive in it, in a matter of a couple of seconds. And after a while, it hardly seemed like work for him anymore. He was now able to recognize that there were positives in any event. Instead of looking for ways things wouldn't work, he was able to say why they could and how to make them work.

And you know what? Every single bit of feedback I said I would give Bob, he got. People did start to ask him for his advice. People did realize he had tremendous knowledge, and did start to respect him for his experience. He did become a role model for people, and they did want him to lead their projects. And he did prove everyone who thought he was a lost cause absolutely wrong.

I'm happy to say that today Bob is an upper level manager, and doing great. Think about that. I was ready to fire the guy! The only thing he needed was training on how to have a positive attitude. No one had ever given this to him before. I was pleased to be able to affect even a small change. I look back on it now and think I was just a few days away from firing him. Bob was not a bad person; he just needed training.

Now that we worked through that one, I want to propose another scenario. Another diamond in the rough was a person that we used to call Mother Teresa.

CHAPTER 18

Don't Worry, Be Happy

In every life we have some trouble,
when you worry you make it double.
Don't worry, be happy.
"Don't Worry, Be Happy" – Bobby McFerrin

Teresa wasn't happy. She worried a lot. Teresa had only been working for me for a few months. She had transferred in from a different area in the company, and I greatly respected her skills and knowledge. She was an excellent technician and was very dedicated to her work. I noticed Teresa started to work longer hours as the months went by and, at the same time, I started seeing a change in her attitude. She was more discouraged in office meetings and less willing to accept change.

When I tried to talk to Teresa about it, she would always bring up things that were happening to other people. She would tell me how John lost his benefits because he wasn't working enough hours and how mad she was at the company for that. She would tell me how Susan didn't get the promotion just because she had a cross word with her manager, etc. After a few minutes listening to this, I realized that almost everything that was turning her attitude sour had nothing to do with her. When I asked her to focus on what was going on with her, she started saying that she was a little disgruntled because she had been working long hours, but then she went right back to describing the woes of other people.

Over the next few days, I noticed something fascinating; something I hadn't really paid attention to before. What I noticed was that people were going into Teresa's office all during the day, sitting down, and talking with her. Of course, previously I thought that they were seeking her advice, because she was very knowledgeable. But then I noticed that the people she was talking to tended to be the very people she voiced concerns about. Hey! It finally occurred to me, she was voicing their concerns.

People liked to come in and talk to her and tell her all their woes for a very simple reason: she would listen. She would offer some advice, but mainly she offered consolation. Therefore, the more consolation she offered, the more people would come to her. Then, once they found out that she had actually voiced their concerns to management, as she did to me, well that did it. She got flooded with more people coming to her; she was now the people's champion. No cause was too small. Teresa was a complaint magnet.

I found out that she was even lovingly referred to as "Mother Teresa" in our office. Presumably, she was named after *the* Mother Teresa.

I went to Teresa and talked to her about this and how it was having a negative effect on her, which of course she rejected as ridiculous. I did learn one thing about Teresa and her habit (no pun intended) of taking on people's ills. She liked it. She liked people seeing her as the person they could come to, that she would be their savior. As a result, she was working a couple of extra hours every day to support this activity, and now it was having a negative effect on her attitude.

I needed to do something with Teresa, but I wasn't quite sure what; then I decided to see if I could apply my formula for changing a person. I remembered the keys were to know what a person wants, show them they can get it, and then give them a taste.

With Teresa, it was no problem knowing what she wanted. In the few months I had been working with her, it was obvious she wanted to leave work on time. Working extra hours was shrinking the time she could spend with her children at home. This was very important to her. So knowing what she desired came without any work at all. Figuring out how to give her a taste of that, well that was not going to be so easy. You see, Teresa rejected the notion that her consultations took very long. She was convinced this was just a few minutes a day.

Normally, I might just try to convince her that if she stopped yakking with people about their troubles all day, she would be able to leave on time. There is the old "Imagine This" technique again, which doesn't work very well. Besides, by asking her to make a change, I was asking her to stop doing something she liked. And without a taste, that would be doomed to fail.

I spoke about this with a friend of mine, and he suggested I just force her to leave work on time. I considered this for a while, but then realized that Teresa was not staying extra hours because she was a slacker. She was staying extra hours because she was a good hard worker and a conscientious employee. She didn't like leaving work until she was caught up, and was willing to work extra hours to do it. If I forced her to leave on time before her work was finished, that was going to taste very sour to her. I had to make sure the "taste" was something that tasted good to her, not bad.

Then, I was in a meeting with a few of the supervisors who reported to me, and I mentioned the problem with Teresa. One of my supervisors said, "Hey, let's give her a paid vacation." "Are you kidding?" I said. "I'm not giving her a vacation for wasting time talking to people about their problems."

"No," he said, "Give her a week's vacation from her troubles. You know, like in that movie *What About Bob*, with Bill Murray. His psychiatrist gave him a vacation from his troubles."

Of course, I was sitting there thinking, "Uh, huh, this is how low we have stooped. Now we are getting our managerial techniques from Bill Murray movies." But, after a few minutes, it didn't seem that farfetched to me anymore. So, I decided I would give her a vacation. That's right; I would give her a paid vacation!

That next day I called Teresa into my office and I said, "Teresa, I'm going to give you a paid vacation." She looked at me rather puzzled, and then I continued on by saying, "Not out of the office, but a paid vacation from people bringing their problems to you. For one week, I'm going to pay you for just your job, and no one is going to be allowed to come into your office to complain about anything. If someone does go into your office, I will stand there and make sure you only talk about work. But for one week you are going to have no one in your office to complain about anything, you are only going to do your job."

Teresa tried to come up with every excuse on why that would not work, but finally agreed after a while. Later that day, in the office meeting I made my announcement that Teresa, for one week, was not allowed to talk to anybody else unless it was strictly about work, and I would be there in the office to make sure. I didn't explain why, I simply said that Teresa is going on a week's vacation from anybody going to her with their problems.

At first, people kind of rolled their eyes and thought Carl was out of his head again; but I decided to see it through. Sure enough, Monday morning, it wasn't one hour after work started that I saw Maggie walk in Teresa's office.

Maggie was short, brash, and loud. That last Friday, when her coworkers complained that they could hardly hear their customers on the phone because Maggie was so loud, I bought Maggie a decibel meter and put it on her desk so she could monitor her own voice. She saw that as the single greatest insult that any human being could possibly inflict on another human being, and apparently couldn't wait to tell Mother Teresa about it.

I walked in and heard the tail end of their conversation about how vicious my actions were. Both Maggie and Teresa tried to pretend it was something about work but when they couldn't fake it, Maggie just left. Other people tried to get in, but were quickly ushered out by either me or one of my supervisors. This went on for the first day and everybody kind of laughed and saw it as a big game.

On the second day, people actually did stay away and I didn't have to chase them out anymore. I then noticed that Teresa was pretty much focusing on her work. By

Wednesday, people weren't coming to her at all anymore. I realized then that previously, no one had come to her for advice on anything that had to do with work. Her time was being constantly consumed by people who wanted to complain about something. I noticed that by Wednesday, Teresa actually left the office about an hour earlier than she used to.

Teresa had been working until 7:00 pm almost consistently and now left about 6:00 pm. By Thursday she left about 5:30 pm. By Friday at the day's end, I noticed that her desk was pretty much cleaned up and all but a couple items on her to-do list were left.

At about 5:00 pm on Friday, Teresa came into my office with a concerned look on her face. She looked around to see if anyone could her us, and said, "Carl, I'd like to talk to you about something. I feel awkward, but was hoping you consider it seriously." "Sure" I said, "what do you need?" Teresa looked at me for a moment, leaned forward, quietly cleared her throat, and said, "Carl, can I have another week's vacation?"

I smiled, and assured her she could have all of the vacation she wanted. All she had to do was take control.

Once again, like with Good ole Bob, I had something. I knew that Teresa wanted to be home with her family. One of the reasons she was feeling disgruntled was because she didn't have enough time to pick up her kids from daycare and that made her sad. Very sad in fact, and she didn't like it. I knew what she wanted without her having to tell me; she wanted to be able to leave work on time. But I also knew that she liked being seen as Mother Teresa in the office. I knew that in order for her to want to leave on time badly enough to make a change, she needed a taste of what it would be like.

She needed a taste, and I gave it to her. It was only a week, but it was good enough. She tasted it, she liked it, and she wanted more. By asking me if she could have another week's vacation, I knew what she was really asking me. She was really asking, "What do I have to do?"

My response was very simple:

Teresa, you can have as many weeks' vacation as you want. All you have to do is realize that every time someone comes to you to talk about their issues, what they are really saying to you is, "Teresa, no matter what you have to do, no matter how important your kids are; it's not as important as the fact that I want to complain about something to you." Then Teresa, all you have to do is make a choice. Is it more important to you to be seen as Mother Teresa? Or is it more important for you to be home with your kids? I'll let you make that choice. If you are concerned about being rude, remember, the person who is interrupting you and making you work longer hours is the one who is really being rude. All you have to do is say, 'I'm sorry, I want to talk to you. Can we talk at lunch or at a break because right now I really need to get these things done?" If people can't respect that, then they are not your friends or are not people you need to worry about being rude to anyway.

I had Teresa wanting to change. She had a desire to leave work on time. She now had a reasonable expectation that that desire was achievable. And she had a taste of it.

By telling her what she had to do to get it, namely to tell people to leave her alone, I taught her how to change. That didn't happen right away. I literally had to teach her what to say, and how to say it. We spent hours in role-plays practicing. Think about it. She didn't know how to say no. I had to teach her. The rest was up to her. And guess what? She changed. Once in a while, Teresa did slip back into her old ways, but then quickly rebounded once she realized she was working longer hours.

In these cases of Good Ole' Bob and Mother Teresa, it was a matter of people having to change their attitude, but not being given the training on how to do that. These are two very simple cases and certainly the steps taken by Bob and Teresa would not be the ones to take in every situation. It does, however, demonstrate that in order to make a change, a person has to both want to **and** know how to.

My advice to anyone who wants to be a successful employee is to start by working on your attitude. To do that, you must stop looking at all the work, and start looking for the opportunity. I suggest by beginning with the steps I used for Good Ole Bob:

Decide what you want and what is important to you.
Make sure it is something you can reasonably achieve.
Give yourself a taste.

To give yourself a taste is the hard part. To be really motivated to do anything, you have to stay away from the "Imagine This" technique, and give yourself a taste.

Here are two easy techniques I am going to get into:

Pretend it.   Restate it.

CHAPTER 19

As Beautiful as You Feel

You've got to get up every morning
with a smile on your face,
And show the world all the love in your heart.
Then people gonna treat you better.
You're gonna find, yes you will,
That you're as beautiful, as you feel.
"Beautiful" – Carole King

Pretend It

I am sure you have heard the phrase "Fake it until you make it." Basically, it says that you can train your mind to accept something just by saying it and acting it constantly. This is actually a very good technique and one I suggest using, if you are looking for a promotion or for people in your office to start seeing you as someone who has leadership ability.

I have found that simply pretending and acting as if you already have achieved what you want can be helpful.

The more you can pretend you already have what you want, the more your attitude and your actions will be tailored to fit with it. Give yourself a taste of it.

I have used this many times myself, and I would like to offer an example.

When I was an employee in an office, I desperately wanted to become a supervisor. So knowing that the concept of "fake it until you make it" can be a positive force, I decided I was going to apply it. One morning I simply decided that I was, in fact, a supervisor. I wasn't going to overstep my bounds, but I was going to imagine that I was a supervisor and start talking and acting as if I already was. I would actually say this to myself in the morning; I am now a supervisor so I need to act that way.

Almost immediately, as I looked at office meetings that were going on, and projects being assigned, I noticed that the more I imagined that I was a supervisor, the easier it was for me to volunteer for projects and be willing to lead focus groups. But I also noticed that I started thinking about things that supervisors do and started doing them myself: Helping a customer who was waiting in the lobby, offering to cover for someone who was out of the office, etc.

One of the things I noticed some good managers often did in our branch was to call other branches and congratulate certain employees if they had received some kind of recognition. If someone in another office had been awarded Employee of the Month, or received a promotion or something, they would often call employees at other branches and say thanks, or just say congratulations.

So, as a "supervisor" myself now, I just started making these calls myself. I did not think I would get in trouble for this or anything, but I went ahead and started reading the newsletters and reading the management monthly reports. Whenever I would see an employee in another branch receive some kind of award or recognition; I would actually call that person and just say, "Hey, this is Carl Van, I am over here at the Sacramento branch. I read that you received the highest number of compliments from customers during the last month, and I just wanted to congratulate you."

Of course, people were usually so excited to here that, and they would go tell their own manager or supervisor that they received a call from some guy named Carl Van in another branch. Everyone over there assuming I was in management.

This is kind of how some managers at our company would encourage each other. Now keep in mind, not all the people in management did this, but some did. And I found myself doing that even though I wasn't a supervisor and even though I wasn't in management. It didn't seem to matter; people still thought it was nice that I was calling. Oftentimes many of the people who received the call just assumed I was already in management because that was something management tended to do.

Now keep in mind that this was not the only thing I would do while pretending I was a supervisor, but just one of many.

About a month into this, I received a call from a manager at another office. (We'll call him Jim, because I couldn't locate him to get his permission to use his real name).

Jim said, "Carl, I just want to let you know that I appreciate the fact that you call my people and congratulate them on stuff. I think that is great and it really boosts morale. So, I wanted to thank you." I told Jim it was no problem and happy to do it. While we were on the phone he asked me, "Hey, by the way, I am working on this one analysis of customer service statistics and I was wondering if you know of anybody who might be interested in your branch in working on the same project."

I told Jim that I would be happy to, and so we just started talking a little bit about it and he sent me some information. It was a very simple project involving trying to analyze complaint calls and the best way to record successful resolutions; something he was going to submit to HR. It took us a very short period of time to do, and he submitted it. HR seemed to like it and our company went with it.

Over the next month or so, I got a couple of calls from Jim, again wanting to bounce some ideas off of me. Then, even a manager at another office called me (He was huge and his last name was Ammerman, but we called him "The Hammer man), who had been talking to Jim, and Jim told him to give me a call because he thought I had some good ideas.

Then, one day a position for a supervisor opened up in Jim's office, and I applied for it. During the interview of course, we broke the ice by talking for a few minutes about that one project we had worked on and some other ideas we had for our company. But then, Jim asked me a question which really floored me. He asked, "Well Carl, I have a question for you. Why would you want to transfer all the way from your branch to this branch, I mean, what is in it for you?"

I told him it wasn't a transfer, that it was a promotion. He was absolutely stunned; Jim had assumed that I was already in supervision or in management in some capacity. When I told him I was still a staff person, he absolutely could not believe it; he had just assumed I was already there. And of course, when it came time to offer the position, who was he going to offer it to? A bunch of other people that had promised they could do a good job, or someone he had actually dealt with and had already seen in the capacity of a management roll?

Needless to say I got the offer for the job, and I attribute almost 100% to the fact that it was because I had already had the mindset of being in that job and started doing things consistent with that.

A giant mistake many employees make is they say to themselves: "Well, once I become a supervisor, then I will start acting like one. Once I become a supervisor I will stop complaining. Once I become a supervisor I will look around to see if I can get involved in projects." They think they have to wait until they have the position in order to demonstrate those attributes. What they don't realize is that by waiting, they are quite literally demonstrating that they don't have those attributes yet. So the technique of pretending that you already have something that you are looking for is a very good way of altering your attitude. After all, as the old and wise guru says, performance is 80% attitude and 20% ability!

The second technique I'll mention is to Restate It.

CHAPTER 20

Say What You Want to Say

Don't stop, to ask. Now you've
found a break to make at last.
You've got to find a way, say what you want to say.
Breakout!
"Breakout" – Swing Out Sister

Restate It

Another great technique is to practice rephrasing the things you say and hear in order to find something positive in it. To be able to say what you want to say is important. Then, just decide you want to try to find something positive if you can, rather than the negative. See if you can break out of some of those bad habits. Below are some comments I have heard employees make rather casually. See if any of them sound familiar.

I have too much work.

My manager gives me all the difficult files.

Customers are always complaining.

If this job was easier, I'd like it better.

No one helps me unless I ask for it.

My job is nerve-racking. One little mistake could cost the company thousands.

The only time I see my supervisor is when I make a mistake.

I always have to go to conferences and review them for everyone else in office meetings.

The customers are so needy. I wish they'd leave me alone.

I'm the only one in my office with any experience.

Here is an exercise. See if you can reword the comments to point out the positive. Keep in mind all of the comments are completely valid. But if you can change them around just a little so they seem positive instead of negative, you are ahead of the game.

In Figure 20.1, I have rewritten the comments as I believe an Exceptional performer would have seen things.

Figure 20.1

I have too much work.
> Well, at least I have job security.

My manager gives me all the difficult files.
> My manager trusts me to handle the difficult files.

Customers are always complaining.
> Customers need my help. That's my job.

If this job was easier, I'd like it better.
> This is a tough job. But, if this job was easier, the company wouldn't need me.

No one helps me unless I ask for it.
> I'm left alone to do my job.

My job is nerve-racking. One little mistake could cost the company thousands.
> I have a job that is important and requires thoughtful care. My company trusts my decisions.

The only time I see my supervisor is when I make a mistake.

My supervisor doesn't hover over me and lets me do my job.

I always have to go to conferences and review them for everyone else in office meetings.
I am trusted to interpret important information and help train others in my office.

The customers are so needy. I wish they'd leave me alone.
The customers are very needy. If they weren't, anyone could do this job.

I'm the only one in my office with any experience.
I am relied upon in my office because of my experience.

Stop Your Whining

Frequently, when I am teaching a training class, there are individuals who want to spend the entire time complaining about their manager. They literally want to spend the entire class trying to prove to me that they have no issue of opportunity for improvement. It is entirely their manager's fault. "Managers are too demanding." "They don't recognize my efforts." "They don't appreciate the hard work that I do." Whatever!

When that happens, I try to bring them around to the fact that no one is perfect. I will say things like, "Well, yeah, your manager's not perfect but, you know what? Your mother's not perfect either and you still love her, don't you? And often that type of comment will get people to realize, "Yeah, nobody is perfect, not even me. And if I can accept and live through the faults of my own mother, then maybe I can forgive my manager just long enough to figure out how to deal with him."

That technique usually works but it did backfire on me one time and I have definitely learned my lesson.

I tried using that technique one time in New Jersey. I said to a guy named Tony in class, "Well, yes, but your mother's not perfect either and you still love her, right." The room went silent, there was a long pause for about ten seconds and Tony looked at me and said, "What did you say about my mother?"

Needless to say, it took me a while to get that class back on track and I did learn my lesson; not every single technique works for every person or even every region of the country. Now I am not saying that we all need to love our managers like we love our mothers, but what I am saying is, every manager has her strengths and every manager has her weaknesses.

It is our job as employees to realize that everyone is different and that we cannot mold our manager into our image. We have to deal with their strengths and weaknesses. Focus on or at least consider their priorities and their situation. Forgive them for their faults and simply find the best way to perform well in that environment. Remember, you can't change other people, but you can change the way you react to them.

Spend just one week pretending you already have what you want, and rewording every negative comment you say or hear, and you will see an immediate change in your attitude toward your responsibilities. Your job satisfaction will go up, and your stress level will go down. Then, if you like the way that tastes, go ahead and indulge. Keep eating up that positive attitude. Don't worry; positive attitude is the ultimate diet. No fat and no carbs!

Remember, attitude is…is…what was that again?

❖ ❖ ❖

Here's Where The Story Ends

It's that little souvenir, of a colorful year,
which makes me smile inside.
Surprise, surprise, surprise, surprise, surprise.
Here's where the story ends.
"Here's Where the Story Ends" – The Sundays

Most exceptional performers have a positive attitude about their job responsibilities. They understand their role. In fact, their attitude about what they think their job is will drive their performance far more than their ability. Sometimes that comes from within, sometimes from their training, and sometimes from their interaction with management. Regardless of where the attitude comes from, it is the most influential part of their performance.

They are not afraid to make mistakes, they are afraid of mediocrity. Their focus is not on protecting themselves; their focus is on improving themselves. To them, making mistakes is an indispensible part of the improvement process. Because of that, they live a much less stressful life then those always worried about never making a mistake.

Exceptional performers are usually people who have a high level of job satisfaction, again because of their attitude. They see the extra responsibilities that their boss lays on them as their boss's outward demonstration that their boss believes in them more than anyone else. They can see the opportunity when everyone else just sees a lot of hard work.

They would rather spend their time trying to figure out how to get something to work, rather than sitting around complaining about why it won't. Usually, they can see the positive side of things, not just the downside.

Exceptional performers relish the opportunity to prove they can do something most people can't.

❖ ❖ ❖

PROFESSIONAL SPEAKING SERVICES

Carl Van is a professional national speaker having delivered presentations throughout the U.S., Canada and the U.K.

His presentation style is upbeat, fast paced and always generates audience participation. He has received numerous recognitions throughout the years, including Most Dynamic Speaker at the national ACE conference.

Mr. Van is qualified to speak on virtually any subject regarding employee performance and customer interaction. Just a few of his Guest Speaking titles include:

General

- Awesome Customer Service: You're Good. You Can Get Better
- How to Avoid Losing Customers
- The Customer Service Standards: 5 Things to Never Forget

- Practical Negotiations: Stop Arguing and Start Agreeing
- Real Life Time Management
- Stress Management: Give Yourself a Break Before You Die.
- Improving your Attitude and Initiative
- Getting People's Cooperation – A Few Easy Steps
- What Customers Hate – And Why We Do It
- If You Can't Say it Simply and Clearly, Then You Don't Know What You're Talking About: Some Business Writing Basics
- Empathy: The Power Tool of Customer Service
- Why Are They Calling Me? Things to do to Reduce Nuisance Calls
- Let Me Do My Job: Simple Steps to get People to be Patient and Let You Do Your Job
- Trust Me: Effective Ways to Gain Credibility
- Saying No: The Right Way (and easy way), or The Wrong Way (the hard way)
- Listening Skills: How to Avoid Missing the Point
- Teamwork: Ways to Reduce the Work Created by Individualism

Management

- Handling Your Difficult Employees (Without Threats and Violence)
- Teaching and Coaching for Supervisors and Managers

- Initiative: How to Develop it in Your Staff
- Stop Wasting Your Time – Practical Time Management for Managers
- Effective Delegation: Why People Hate It When You Delegate, and How to Change That
- Managing Change
- Interviewing and Hiring Exceptional Performers
- Motivating Your Team
- How to Make Sure Your Employees get the Most out of Training
- Inspiring Employees to Improve Themselves

For a free DVD, please visit
www.CarlVan.org or call 504-393-4570.

"Like" Carl Van on www.Facebook.com/
CarlVanSpeaker for updates.

Follow Carl Van on www.Twitter.com/CarlVanSpeaker

IN-PERSON TRAINING SERVICES

Carl Van is President & CEO of an international training company that delivers high quality training directly to customers at their locations. He is the author of over 75 technical and soft skill courses that have been delivered to over 100,000 employees throughout the U.S, Canada and the U.K.

Just a few titles of his programs include:

Employee Soft-Skill

- Real-Life Time Management for Employees
- The 8 Characteristics of the Awesome Employee
- Negotiation Training
- Conflict Resolution
- Awesome Customer Service
- Managing the Telephone
- Attitude & Initiative Training for the Employee
- Empathy & Listening Skills
- Employee Organization – Managing the Desk
- Prepare for Promotion – Employee Leadership Training
- Teamwork Basics – No Employee is an Island
- Interpersonal Skills – Improving Team Member Relations

- Effective Recorded Statements
- Business Writing Skills for Employees
- Beating Anxiety and Dealing with Anger – Help for the New Employee

Manager Soft-Skill

- Time Management for Supervisors and Managers
- Coaching and Teaching for Supervisors and Managers
- Keys to Effective Presentations
- Teaching Your Employees the 8 Characteristics of Awesome Employees
- Motivating Your Team
- Handling Difficult Employees
- The New Supervisor
- Interviewing and Hiring Exceptional Performers
- Delegation Training for Supervisors and Managers
- Managing Change
- Team Training
- Leadership Skills for Supervisors and Managers
- Preparing Effective Performance Appraisals
- Managing the Highly Technical Employee

For more information and a free catalog of courses, please visit www.InsuranceInstitute.com or call 504-393-4570.

ON-LINE TRAINING SERVICES

Carl Van is President and owner of an on-line website that delivers high quality training through streaming video that employees can access anywhere in the world.

He is also available to write, direct and present training courses specific to an individual company or industry. He wrote and presented a customer service course on DVD for a national company which was rolled out to all 18,000 line employees.

He is the designer, author and presenter of four on-line video training courses:

- Exceptional Claims Customer Service
- Negotiation Skills for the Claims Professional
- Real-Life Time Management for Claims
- Critical Thinking for Claims

For more information, visit www.
ClaimsEducationOnLine.com.

EDUCATIONAL ARTICLES BY CARL VAN

Carl Van is owner and publisher of his own educational magazine, and is the author of numerous articles that have appeared in various periodicals.

Just a sample of articles written by Carl Van:

Van, Carl "Negotiation – Understanding the Other Point of View." Promotional Consultant Today. www.promotionalconsultanttoday.org April, 2011

Van, Carl "Gaining Cooperation."

Audiology Advance Magazine. www.audiology.advanceweb.com April, 2011

Pharmacy Week. www.pharmacyweek.com April, 2011

Print Wear Magazine. www.printwearmag.com April, 2011

The Real Estate Professional Magazine. www.therealestatepro.com April, 2011

Weekly Article Magazine. www.WeeklyArticle.com March 2011.

Industrial Supply Magazine. www.industrialsupplymagazine.com March, 2011.

Furniture World Magazine. www.Furninfo.com March 2011.

Contact Professional. www.ContactProfessional.com March 2011.

Promotional Consultants Today. www. PromotionalConsultantToday.org; March, 2011.

Van, Carl "Three Maxims for Successful Negotiation." Dealer Marketing Magazine www.DealerMarketing.com March 2011.

Van, Carl. "Our Life's Work." Property Casualty 360. www.PropertyCasualty360.com January, 2011.

Van, Carl. "The Five Standards of Great Claims Organizations." Property Casualty 360. www. PropertyCasualty360.com February, 2011.

Van, Carl. "Online Claims Training Program Expands: Time Management for Claims added to curriculum." Claims Education Magazine. www.claimseducationmagazine. com Fall 2010.

Van, Carl. "5th Annual Claims Education Conference Earns Superbowl Status." Claims Education Magazine. Summer 2010: Pg. 1.

Van, Carl. "While Others Wait, Bold Companies Invest in Training." Subrogator. Winter 2010: Pg. 102.

Van, Carl. "While Others Wait, Bold Companies Invest in Training Part III." <u>Claims Education Magazine</u>. Spring 2010: Pg. 1.

Van, Carl. "While Others Wait, Bold Companies Invest in Training Part II." <u>Claims Education Magazine.</u> December 2009- Vol. 6, No. 6: Pg. 1.

Van, Carl. "While Others Wait, Some Invest in Training." <u>Claims Education Magazine.</u> October/November 2009- Vol. 6, No. 5: Pg. 3

Van, Carl. "Tips on Taking Statements & Information Gathering." <u>Claims Education Magazine.</u> October/ November 2009- Vol. 6, No. 5: Pg. 1.

Van, Carl. "Placing the Bets." <u>Claims Education Magazine.</u> March/April 2009- Vol. 6, No. 2: Pg. 1.

Van, Carl. "Lesson in Customer Service & Attitude." <u>Claims Education Magazine. </u>January/February 2009- Vol. 6, No. 1: Pg. 1.

Van, Carl. "Saying It the Right Way." <u>Claims Education Magazine.</u> Fall 2008- Vol. 5, No. 4: Pg. 8.

Van, Carl. "Critical Thinking Part Three." <u>Claims Education Magazine</u>. Summer 2008- Vol. 5, No. 3: Pg. 4.

Van, Carl. "Critical Thinking Part Two." <u>Claims Education Magazine</u>. Spring 2008- Vol. 5, No. 2: Pg. 4.

Van, Carl. "Critical Thinking Part One." <u>Claims Education Magazine</u>. Winter 2008- Vol. 5, No. 1: Pg. 4.

Van, Carl. "Desire for Excellence." <u>Claims Education Magazine</u>. Fall 2007- Vol. 4, No. 4: Pg. 14.

Van, Carl. "Building a Claim Team." <u>Claims</u>. October 2005.

Van, Carl. "In Search of Initiative." <u>Claims</u>. September 2005.

Van, Carl. "A Velvet Hammer Can Expedite Negotiations." <u>Claims Education Magazine</u>. Summer 2005- Vol. 1, No. 1: Pg. 10.

Van, Carl. "Claims Management: Desire for Excellence." <u>Claims</u>. July 2005.

Van, Carl. "Empathizing with Customers." <u>Claims</u>. June 2005.

Van, Carl. "Never Stop Learning." <u>Claims</u>. May 2005.

Van, Carl. "Interpersonal Skills: Avoid the Hammer." <u>Claims</u>. April 2005.

Van, Carl. "Secrets of Successful Time Management." <u>Claims.</u> March 2005.

Van, Carl. "Attitude." <u>Claims Magazine</u>. February 2005: Pg. 10.

Van, Carl. "Tend to Your Garden: A Vision of Claims Education." <u>Claims.</u> February 2003: Pg. 34.

Van, Carl. "Adjusters: How not to Drive Away Clients." <u>National Underwriter</u>. September 24, 2001.

Van, Carl & Sue Tarrach. "The 8 Characteristics of Awesome Adjusters." <u>Claims.</u> December 1996.

Carl Van is available for consulting, training and guest speaking appearances. To contact Mr. Van, call 504-393-4570 or visit:

www.CarlVan.org
www.Facebook.com/CarlVanSpeaker
www.Linkedin.com/CarlVan (Carl Van - Awesome Adjuster group)

ARTICLES FEATURING CARL VAN

Mr. Van has been the subject of numerous articles outlining his services and educational philosophy. A few are:

Gilkey, Eric. "Strategies for Gaining Cooperation." <u>IASIU</u>. Monday, September 13, 2010: Pg. 4.

Henry, Susan, and Mary Anne Medina. "Evaluating Adjuster Performance." <u>Claims</u>. August 2010: Pg. 36.

Gilkey, Eric. "Hiring and Motivating the Right People." <u>NASP Daily News</u>, November 3, 2009: Pg. 6.

"Permission to Say, 'I'm Sorry.'" <u>Canadian Underwriter</u>. September 1, 2008.

Aznoff, Dan. "Fair Oaks Students Take Speaker's Advice to Heart for Positive Attitude." <u>The Sacramento Bee.</u> April 12, 2007: City Section, Pg. G5.

Friedman, Sam. "WC Claimants 'Not the Enemy,' Trainer says." <u>National Underwriter.</u> September 24, 2001.

Prochaska, Paul. "Awesome Adjusting Revisited: A Return to Customer Service." <u>Claims.</u> February, 2000.

Hays, Daniel. "Being Kinder and Gentler Pays Off: Insurance Claims is a Customer Service Business." <u>Claims.</u> December 2000: Pg. 56.

Carl Van is available for consulting, training and guest speaking appearances. To contact Mr. Van, call 504-393-4570 or visit:

www.CarlVan.org
www.Facebook.com/CarlVanSpeaker
www.Linkedin.com/CarlVan (Carl Van - Awesome Adjuster group)

BOOKS BY CARL VAN

Van, Carl. <u>The 8 Characteristics of the Awesome Adjuster</u>. Published by Arthur Hardy Enterprises, Inc., ISBN 0-930892-66-6 (Metairie, LA) Copyright © 2005

Van, Carl. <u>Gaining Cooperation: Some Simple Steps to Getting Customers to do What You Want Them to do</u>. Published by International Insurance Institute, Inc., ISBN 1456334107 & 13-9781456334109 (New Orleans, LA) Copyright © 2011

Van, Carl. <u>Attitude, Ability and the 80-20 Rule</u>. Published by International Insurance Institute, Inc., (New Orleans, LA) Copyright © 2011

Coming Soon:

Van, Carl and Hinz, Debra. <u>Gaining Cooperation: 3 Easy Steps to Getting Injured Workers to do What you Want Them to do</u>. Published by International Insurance Institute, Inc., (New Orleans, LA) Copyright © 2011

Van, Carl and Wimsatt, Laura. <u>The Claims Cookbook: A Culinary Guide to Job Satisfaction.</u> Published by International Insurance Institute, Inc., (New Orleans, LA) Copyright © 2011

Van, Carl. <u>Hiring Excellent Employees – Givers vs. Takers</u>. Published by International Insurance Institute, Inc., (New Orleans, LA) Copyright © 2011

Van, Carl. <u>Critical Thinking for the Claims Professional</u> Published by International Insurance Institute, Inc., (New Orleans, LA) Copyright © 2011

Van, Carl. <u>The 8 Characteristics of the Awesome Employee</u>. To be published in 2012.

Carl Van is available for consulting, training and guest speaking appearances. To contact Mr. Van, call 504-393-4570 or visit:

www.CarlVan.org
www.Facebook.com/CarlVanSpeaker
www.Linkedin.com/CarlVan (Carl Van - Awesome Adjuster group)

CONTACT CARL VAN

Carl Van is available for consulting, training and guest speaking appearances. To contact Mr. Van, call 504-393-4570 or find him at any of the following:

www.CarlVan.org
www.Facebook.com/CarlVanSpeaker
www.Linkedin.com/CarlVan   (Carl Van – Awesome Adjuster group)
www.Twitter.com/CarlVanSpeaker
www.ClaimsEducationMagazine.com
www.ClaimsEducationConference.com
www.ClaimsExecutiveAcademy.com
www.ClaimsManagerAcademy.com
www.ClaimsSkillsAcademy.com
www.ClaimsProfessionalBooks.com
www.ClaimsEducationOnLine.com
www.InsuranceInstitute.com

Made in the USA
Charleston, SC
13 July 2011